M000228682

'Claud Jackson is a ma_____ _____ __ _____ that he walked into Spoonful Café to do Alpha with our church over seven years ago. Since then, he has become a treasured friend and we have witnessed his life being transformed by Jesus. We hope that you too will catch afresh the hope of the gospel as you journey through Claud's story.'
David and Rachel Cooke, Holy Trinity Barnes

'Claud Jackson led a life of poverty, abuse, drug dealing and violence before encountering Jesus Christ. He is a hugely talented writer who tells his own heart-wrenching story beautifully. Now his life is on a completely different path and, by the end, his readers are left inspired and full of hope.'
Nicky Gumbel, Vicar, Holy Trinity Brompton

'Anyone who thinks that they might be too deeply involved in a lifestyle of crime and deceit, resulting in an inner hollowness, will be inspired that total transformation is possible. Claud today is a gentle giant who knows God has a plan for his life. Make sure you read this and discover how God can radically change you too.'
Emmy Wilson, Curate, Holy Trinity Brompton

Claud Jackson is an ex-drug dealer turned trainee vicar. Growing up in south London, Claud's childhood was one of conflict and confusion as he struggled to find good role models to inspire good choices. A life of crime became inevitable. Claud's reputation was growing rapidly among the criminal fraternity and the police alike until an encounter with Jesus changed everything. Coming to faith through Alpha, Claud went on to join the staff team of Holy Trinity Brompton, where he is currently an ordinand, studying theology at St Mellitus while training for ordination. He hopes to inspire the next generation to know that Jesus offers something drugs, reputation and money can't buy: true freedom. *Guns to God* is his first book.

CLAUD JACKSON

GUNS TO GOD

MY JOURNEY FROM DRUG DEALING TO DELIVERANCE

First published in Great Britain in 2021

Society for Promoting Christian Knowledge
36 Causton Street
London SW1P 4ST
www.spck.org.uk

Copyright © Claud Jackson 2021

All rights reserved. No part of this book may be reproduced or transmitted in any form or by any means, electronic or mechanical, including photocopying, recording, or by any information storage and retrieval system, without permission in writing from the publisher.

SPCK does not necessarily endorse the individual views contained in its publications.

Scripture quotations are taken from The Holy Bible, New International Version (Anglicized edition). Copyright © 1979, 1984, 2011 by Biblica. Used by permission of Hodder & Stoughton Ltd, an Hachette UK company. All rights reserved. 'NIV' is a registered trademark of Biblica. UK trademark number 1448790.

British Library Cataloguing-in-Publication Data
A catalogue record for this book is available from the British Library

ISBN 978–0–281–08494–4
eBook ISBN 978–0–281–08495–1

1 3 5 7 9 10 8 6 4 2

Typeset by Manila Typesetting Company
Printed and bound in Great Britain by Jellyfish Print Solutions
Subsequently digitally printed in Great Britain

eBook by Manila Typesetting Company

Produced on paper from sustainable forests

This book is dedicated to God,
who 'so loved the world that he gave his one and only Son,
that whoever believes in him shall not perish
but have eternal life'
(John 3.16)

FOREWORD

I read this book in one day. It is a story that grips the reader from start to finish. I grew up reading about men and women of remarkable faith: Nicky Cruz, Corrie ten Boom, Jackie Pullinger, Brother Yun and many more. Those stories have stuck with me throughout my life as I draw on them for not only the inspiration of faith but also a broader insight that takes me beyond my own surroundings and culture to a different world. In reading Claud's story, I believe that *Guns to God* will join this faithful chorus of witnesses to God's almighty work – and it is a story that is still being told.

I've known Claud for a number of years and have been privileged to walk with him on the latest part of his journey. The Claud you meet in this book is the person I know in real life: a deeply loyal, passionate man, who wears his heart on his sleeve. Claud perceives the world clearly and is gifted in terms of his ability to understand the nuances of a situation. In reading his story you will see that he has had a lifetime of working out his place within it. Each chapter describes something of his experience that has shaped the person he has become today.

It is rare that we ever fully understand other people, to know completely their experiences, history and shaping events. In this book, Claud allows us to be part of his story, sharing his struggles and successes, and the questions they have forced him to face. You will learn more about Claud than would otherwise be possible: things that make you think differently about the author, what family is, the place of community in shaping character and the world in general.

Claud offers us *his* story. He has not sought to glamorize what took place or falsify the picture. Rather, he recounts his own story of transformation. There will be parts that are difficult to read: pages where you wish others had responded to Claud differently, and pages where you wish Claud had responded differently. This is because it is a true story, reflecting success and mistake, regret and restoration. Every person faces the temptation to sell their best selves to the world, but it is only when we allow the guard to drop that we truly discover something new. Claud has allowed his guard to drop in this book.

This story is about wanting to hide. From hurt, from responsibility, from hope. It is also about searching: 'I was searching for freedom, some form of escape . . . I needed something stronger.' It is this honesty that reached into my heart as I read, and I hope it will reach into your heart also. As you read, it will draw you into reflecting on the impact that family, community and faith can have. There is something stronger that can transform, a God who will do all he can for you to notice his presence. In Claud's search for connection, we can place our own story.

My own story is very different from Claud's: in childhood and schooling, employment and opportunity, our lives have taken us to very different places. We are from the same country and are a similar age, but in reading Claud's story, it felt like I had entered a different world. Yet we are good friends and the richness of what we have in common is clear in what holds our friendship together. What Claud describes in this book, and what I have experienced similarly, is the love of Jesus Christ. In Jesus, all barriers and boundaries are surpassed. We are all one in Christ Jesus. Today Claud and I enjoy a friendship that is secured in our friendship with him. Being a friend of Jesus can make you a social misfit (it has always been thus), but as Claud writes, 'at least we "fit" together'.

As I read this book, I was reminded of the prayer of Paul for the Ephesians (3.17b–19):

> And I pray that you, being rooted and established in love, may have power, together with all the Lord's holy people, to grasp how wide and long and high and deep is the love of Christ, and to know this love that surpasses knowledge – that you may be filled to the measure of all the fullness of God.

Claud's story is one of the height and depth of the love of Christ. I recommend this book to all: for those who love Jesus, and those who are yet to discover his love. Whether you read it in a day or take your time over it, there is a challenge in these pages to see the work of God in one man's life, and the hand of God over all our lives.

Russell Winfield
Dean, St Mellitus College

IT WAS A REMARKABLE CHANGE THAT NOBODY COULD HAVE SEEN COMING, LEAST OF ALL ME.

INTRODUCTION

I was six years old when I first held a gun in my hands. Gathered in our small living room in London, I looked down at the cold, hard metal, somehow feeling as if I belonged, like maybe this power could protect me. Now, more than 30 years later, I find myself working as a curate for a church, studying theology at Bible college and preparing to return to neighbourhoods just like the one my six-year-old self found himself standing in, but this time holding a Bible.

It was a remarkable change that nobody could have seen coming, least of all me. Prior to my first encounter with Jesus I lived a life that would be considered unimaginable to most, difficult to many and rewarding to few. My only focus was my own selfish financial gain, and I would stop at little to get it. Whether being part of London's drug trade from the age of 15, or avoiding police capture and outsmarting rivals on the gritty city streets, so long as I was making money I simply didn't care about the consequences or serious harm that I was causing to myself and others. I didn't know then what I know now: money cannot buy love.

Though I began documenting my thoughts and feelings over a decade ago – while I was right in the middle of my criminal career – writing this book has caused me to relive many truths over and over again. Any financial wealth I gained then was far outweighed by the hardship and heartbreak I endured. In pursuit of notoriety, I suffered depression, wrestled anxiety and lived with paranoia; a social outcast, I was living with an inner emptiness that longed for fulfilment. Soon I found myself pursuing a dream that didn't even exist. Living by the second, gambling everything, treating life like a dice roll, I didn't care if I won or lost. Crashing my way through life, I was fighting to enjoy the highs while dreading the lows. The good times were short-lived. The bad times will be remembered for ever. But the best was yet to come.

In all this mess I encountered Jesus, and things would never be the same again. Giving my life to him has not rid me of all doubt, worry and confusion. I still make plenty of mistakes and grapple with various questions, but by God's truly amazing grace I have been set free.

If, like me, you find yourself in a messy situation – a situation so dark and so bleak that you can't see a way out – I hope my story will encourage you to see that the Lord can use everything that has happened for his glory; he has a plan and a purpose for your life.

I have tried to recount my story of transformation – or, rather, Jesus' transformation of my life – as clearly as possible. Naturally, some of these memories are blurrier than others. As the naturalist W. H. Hudson wrote in his autobiography *Far Away and Long Ago* (1982):

When a person endeavours to recall his early life in its entirety, he finds it is not possible . . . It is easy to fall into the delusion that the few things thus distinctly remembered and visualised are precisely those which were most important in our life and that account were saved by memory. Unconscious artistry sneaks in to erase unseemly lines and blots, to retouch, colour, shade and falsify the picture.

I will try at every turn not to 'falsify the picture', but regardless of the memories and experiences recalled here, I pray that one truth stands as you read on: God's truly amazing grace took a once successful London drug-dealing street trader all the way from deliveries to deliverance, from guns to God. This is my story.

MY WHOLE EARLY
CHILDHOOD WAS
LIVED ON THE EDGE,
JUST TREADING ON
EGGSHELLS.

CHAPTER ONE

I put my fingers into my ears, closed my eyes and began to hum. I must have been four at the time, so I had little understanding of what was going on, but still I knew this was the only way to drown out the core-cracking, soul-shuddering sounds of my parents' arguments. In later life I would learn about a thousand different childhoods – some where children played with toy soldiers, others where children were forced to fight on the frontline as child soldiers – but for me, like so many others, violence at home was all I had ever known.

Born in Clapham, the youngest of six siblings, those early years were spent living in Tooting, which back then was a working-class area where you were brought up to respect your elders. Like me, my mother was a true Londoner: born in south London and brought up in Camberwell. My father, however, was born and grew up in Jamaica. He had a rough exterior and an even rougher hand; he was the sort of man who could put fear into anyone just by looking at them. He carried the presence of a silverback gorilla: aggressive and unpredictable. His violent behaviour would regularly boil over into every area of our lives.

Though outside my house was generally quite friendly, with neighbours regularly saying hello to one another, inside the atmosphere was always cold. In part due to his own upbringing, my dad was abusively controlling, incredibly strict and very, very strong. Even from those early years, I remember knowing that my dad would never back down, not from anything or anyone. Just conversing with my father could and often *would* end in disagreement, an argument or worse. We all learnt to say very little while in his presence. My whole early childhood was lived on the edge, just treading on eggshells.

I lived in fear, not knowing when the constant arguing would tip over into violence, but when it did, my father wouldn't think twice about striking out at my mum, siblings and me with the closest thing he could get his hands on. His weapon of choice was usually the cane.

The cane was an old stick of bamboo, about four feet in length and less than an inch wide. You could hear it whistle as it cut through the air before viciously arriving at its desired destination. The sound of it is seared into my memory, along with a feeling I can never shake: the feeling of being summoned by my father and ordered to fetch the cane.

Being sent to get that cane was so degrading. I was always left feeling humiliated, vulnerable and worthless. I would be forced to walk past other members of my family waiting en route in the hallway to intercept me, crying and pleading with me not to fetch it. They would look at me teary-eyed and beg me to say that I couldn't find it. The condemnation I felt for 'betraying' my siblings like this was emotionally inescapable. It would play over and over in my head for days afterwards. Every time I got into bed and closed my eyes, I would relive the whole thing. It was traumatizing. I wasn't even five years old.

I remember one time being sent to get the cane and returning to my father empty-handed. Riddled with guilt and shaking with fear, I told him that the cane was nowhere to be found. The look my father gave me in return will stay with me for ever. I can still remember the deep blackness of his pupils as they effortlessly cut through the soft innocent fabric of my heart and landed bluntly in my soul. I knew then that if I didn't immediately return with the bamboo stick in hand, I would be next in line to meet the 'executioner'.

One day I was playing in my elder brothers' room, which was on the ground floor at the back of the house, when I heard a commotion coming from the other side. Entering the living room, I saw that my father had arrived home from work and a few of my siblings were excitedly gathering around him. He was smiling. Hurrying towards my siblings, I was met halfway by a beautiful little thing bounding about in excitement: we'd got a puppy.

It couldn't have been older than a few months. Black with brown socks, it had a long tail and looked a little bit like an Alsatian. Instantly, my young mind filled with all the adventures we would have together, how much fun it would be going for walks and playing catch with our newest member of the family. Maybe it already knew how to play Frisbee like the dogs I had seen on the television . . .

Sadly, I couldn't have been more wrong. That same night the puppy was immediately taken away and locked in the kitchen. The following days were a living nightmare, for the puppy and for me. If somehow the puppy managed to escape and make its way into the house, it would be beaten. If it cried or had an accident, it would be beaten again and kicked out into the garden until my mother let it back in, pleading with it not to make any more noise.

I couldn't watch as my father beat the puppy; I would run to the furthest room in the house, covering my ears. But it wasn't just the beatings that had an impact on me; it was the neglect. We were never allowed to bond with the puppy, and it was forced to live off leftovers from our own dinner. By the time it grew into an adult dog, it was locked in the garden for good. Summer, spring, autumn and winter, the innocent animal was forced to live outdoors, chained and restrained.

In many ways my father was keeping my mother chained too. My mum would wake up around 5 a.m. every day just to cook breakfast for him and then prepare his lunch for work. While preparing breakfast for the rest of the family, she would get my siblings and me ready for school. She continued this routine for almost 30 years. Looking back now, I'm not sure she had much choice.

I remember one morning I was watching cartoons on my bed, which was still in my parents' room at the time. My mother had just finished her usual routine, seeing my father off to work and my siblings off to school. Still too young to go, I stayed behind. My mother was just about to begin her housework when I asked her if she could sit with me and watch cartoons for a short while. She explained that she couldn't, she had to do the housework, but I pleaded with her over and over just to sit with me for a bit. Eventually she gave in, reluctantly placing the furniture polish and duster down and hesitantly making her way over to sit next to me on the bed. With my mother snuggled up next to me I felt so happy. She had only been sitting with me for a few short minutes when we heard the front door open and slam shut. Seconds later my father appeared in the doorway to the bedroom. I smiled at him. He didn't return the gesture. Instead he looked over at my mother and charged towards her, shouting at the top of his voice. The next thing I knew, she was laying over me, her right arm raised to protect herself from the flurry of physical abuse that my father had begun to savagely deliver. I can still hear my mother pleading for him to stop, but he continued raining down blows on her. He was relentless; each thump landed with the bass of a kick drum. There was nothing I could do except cry. I cried so heavily that I lost my breath. Then it was all over just as suddenly as it had started. My father turned around and marched out of the room, leaving my mother and me in tears. Then I heard the front door open and slam shut again.

Scared and speechless, I looked at my mother as she took a couple of seconds to compose herself. Still visibly upset, she asked me, 'Are you OK?'

I stared on as she got up from the bed, picked up the furniture polish and casually continued to dust. A while later I mustered the courage to ask, 'Why did Daddy hit you?'

'Oh,' she replied. 'He just forgot something.'

Why had my father aggressively attacked my mother because *he* had forgotten something? I couldn't get my head around it. Then again, I was only four.

According to one of my brothers, domestic violence was 'the norm during the eighties', yet the thought of my father hitting my mother or one of my siblings never felt normal to me. Though I've learnt in later life that there is nothing 'normal' about domestic violence, sadly it is still commonplace in many people's lives. According to the Office for National Statistics (2019), approximately 2.4 million adults aged 16 to 74 experienced domestic abuse in the year ending March 2019. That's around 786,000 men and 1.6 million women. And it doesn't just come in the form of physical violence. SafeLives, the UK-wide charity dedicated to ending domestic abuse, notes that the UK government's definition in 2020 was:

> any incident or pattern of incidents of controlling, coercive, threatening behaviour, violence or abuse between those aged 16 or over who are, or have been, intimate partners or family members regardless of gender or sexuality. The abuse can encompass but is not limited to psychological, physical, sexual, financial, emotional.

As a young boy, I didn't have the language to understand that my father's behaviour was abusive. And not just emotionally and physically but also *spiritually*. Over time, my father's erratically unpredictable ways began to overflow into other areas of our lives. He would sometimes leave random items lying around the house in peculiar places, which I later learnt were part of some sort of obeah practice.

Late one evening, two African witch doctors accompanied by two women randomly turned up at the front door. We later discovered that my father had invited them. Once inside they would practise all sorts of rituals. Sometimes our whole family would be expected to take part in the practices, but most of the time they would just use me because I was considered 'an innocent infant'. I remember being called into a room by my father, where he and two witch doctors were waiting. In the centre of the room was a single wooden chair. I was told by one of the witch doctors in his thick African accent, '*Sit*.' I fearfully followed his instructions as a bucket of dark, dirty water was thrust on to my lap and a blanket thrown over my head, covering me from head to toe. I started to panic. Then I heard the same voice bark: 'Look into the bucket; tell me what you see.' At first, I hesitated. I didn't want to do it.

'Claud,' my father boomed. 'Look into the bucket and tell the man what you see.'

'Yes, look into the bucket,' the African accent ordered urgently.

Reluctantly, I gave in. Taking a deep breath, I looked into the bucket and told them exactly what I saw. The blanket was then swiftly removed from my head and the bucket taken from my lap. I looked up and saw the sincere surprise on the witch doctor's face as his assistant hurried me out of the room. The door was swiftly shut behind me and no more was ever said.

I don't know why or where it all began for my father, but obeah, a form of witchcraft, was practised heavily during the era of slavery and brought to the Caribbean by practising African slaves. Soon, Kingston in Jamaica was considered by many to be the capital for obeah witchcraft. At the same time, Jamaica is a highly religious country, with Christianity dominating many aspects of Jamaican life. Some research even suggests that the country has the highest ratio of churches to people in the whole world, with Christianity practised everywhere in Jamaica, from small, wooden meeting halls to mega-churches with congregations numbering into the thousands. From a faith perspective, the country could be considered contradictory and controversial. The same confusion ran through my father and spilled out into our family life. One day he would tell us that he was flying some of his relatives over from Jamaica who were specialist witch doctors and the next day he would be saying grace at the dinner table and reading aloud from his Bible. His teachings felt as sporadic and unstable as his behaviour and very soon I began to feel increasingly anxious and unsettled.

The nights were the worst and I grew very fearful of the dark. When it was time for bed, my mother would kiss me goodnight and then I would snuggle deep down under the covers, curling my body into a small ball and pulling the duvet all the way up over my ears. Only then would I feel safe enough to fall asleep. Curled up under this makeshift shield was the only way I could make it through each night. It felt as though the darkness was lingering over me; that there was no way to escape the black cloud. I hadn't even started primary school, but my anxieties were developing rapidly.

When my father was at work and my siblings were at school, I would follow my mum around the house as she did the housework, just happy to be in her company. As soon as I was alone, I would become overwhelmingly aware that I was actually on my own and instantly run out of the room to be in the company of others. The line between fantasy and reality for children is already thin, with imaginary play often feeling as real as anything else. Imaginary monsters under the bed or in the dark are as frightening as a real threat to children with a 'normal' childhood, never mind one involving hostility, violence, poverty and witchcraft.

It was around the age of five that I realized my father was engaging in all sorts of spirituality. It was also at this age that I felt the same question pressing on my heart again and again. I finally mustered up the courage to ask my mother, 'Who is God?'

My siblings and I weren't brought up as practising Christians, despite my father's sporadic declarations that we were going to go 'to service' – which consisted of him driving all of us three and a half hours to a hall in Birmingham for a bizarre meeting of around 200 people – so I don't really know where my question about God came from. All I knew was that I was filled with an overwhelming need to find out who he was.

Though my relationship with my dad was complex, torn between admiring and despising his ox-like strength, my relationship with my mum was simple: I loved her and she loved me. Being the youngest child of six and having a similar sense of humour, we used to be very close. Even in the midst of everything she went through, she would always put her children first. She used to smoke 20 cigarettes a day to calm her nerves, but I can still remember times when she'd go without them just to buy us dinner.

We were a poor family, so it may seem strange to read that my mother made sure I had every toy I ever wanted, from Action Force and Thundercats to literally hundreds of American wrestling figurines. Looking back, I think this was my mother's way of cushioning me from the terrible pain and darkness that filled our lives on a daily basis. She wasn't hugely physically affectionate, so buying me gifts was her way of showing me that she loved me. Playing with the toys that she managed to purchase brought me a great deal of comfort. That's all I used to do as a child, play with my toys one after another. Meanwhile my mother went without. She struggled to pay the bills, struggled to afford dinner, struggled to buy our school uniforms, struggled to buy our shoes, but somehow she managed to do it all and made sure we never went without. I can honestly say that my mother is the strongest person I have ever met. She's lived a life filled with nothing but pain, but has kept going regardless.

Unfortunately, as a result of the lifestyle she had to live, my mother had to deal with many issues and, as is always the case when journeying with loved ones, her issues have become my own. That's what happens in childhood: you inherit all sorts of issues from your parents and your siblings around you. From my father's stubbornness and strength to my mother's sensitivity and determination, I soaked up my surroundings like a dry sponge does water. The good, the bad and the ugly. What I was only beginning to understand then was that my brother's influence was about to change the course of my life for ever.

MOST SIX-YEAR-OLD BOYS WANT TO BE A FIREMAN OR A FOOTBALLER, BUT NOT ME. I WANTED TO BE A STREET ICON, A GANGSTER, JUST LIKE MY BROTHER.

CHAPTER TWO

I looked down at the jet-black 9-mm handgun held in my six-year-old hands. I had seen the same style of gun in many action movies by this point, but never in real life. I handed it back to my eldest brother, only then noticing the thick shoelace scar that ran across the top of his left hand. A thousand questions ran through my mind: how had he got it? Was it an old stab wound? Did he get it in a fight? And, if so, who could possibly have been brave enough to challenge my eldest brother?

To say that my brother's influence on me had a great impact would be an understatement. In my young eyes, he was the coolest guy I had ever seen. Easily noticeable with his distinctive light-brown skin and his disarming dark-brown eyes, his style was effortless. Mixed with his edgy exterior was an undeniable charisma that would immediately disarm anyone who came in contact with him. I wanted to be just like him when I grew up. Most six-year-old boys want to be a fireman or a footballer, but not me. I wanted to be a street icon, a gangster, just like my brother.

My brothers and I shared many fun times growing up, often going for bike rides over Tooting Bec Common with a handful of local kids from the area. I remember riding up a gravel track, pedalling as fast as my little legs would go in an attempt to keep up with the older ones. Most of the time I would end up at the back of the pack. This one time, the dust from the track filled the air around us as we pedalled and the dust from the boy's bike in front of me began to cloud my vision. Before long I fell, my hands crashing into the sharp, hard gravel, cutting open my right palm. My brothers stopped instantly, gathering around me as I cried; there was so much blood it looked as if I was wearing a red glove. I still have a scar on the palm of my hand and to this day, every time I look at it I smile, remembering how very apologetic the kid riding in front of me was afterwards. Maybe he was just genuinely really sorry, but the chances are he knew all about my eldest brother's reputation.

My brother's street reputation echoed his menacing behaviour. He and his friends were an intimidating gang of thugs who wouldn't hesitate to rob, steal or simply take whatever they wanted whenever they wanted it. My brother's friends respected him greatly and some even called him Sinbad. Originally, Sinbad was a fictional sailor of Eastern origin, who would adventure throughout the seas, going to magical places and always coming home with stories. Not only would my eldest brother come home with stories but he also carried a curved knife that reminded his friends of the type of curved sword that Sinbad the sailor was known to carry. My brother learnt to defend himself from an early age simply because he had to. He left our family home in his early teens and managed to survive on his own on the streets. One of the ways he did this was through boxing, with him learning basic skills that were then developed through random but regular street fights. He knew how to throw a devastating knockout punch and I once saw him knock a grown man out completely with a single punch – right in front of our mother.

Inspired by my brother's fondness for boxing, I remember when my three older brothers rearranged the furniture in their bedroom to resemble a boxing ring. Pitted against the brother closest to me in age, I was encouraged to fist fight. Still very young and with this brother a good five years older than me, I became overwhelmed with panic and turned to grab the darts out of the dartboard hanging behind me. Facing my opponent, I took aim and watched as fear filled my brother's eyes. He pleaded with me to stop, but my two other brothers watched on, challenging my commitment to the threat. I threw the first dart, which landed on the floor, missing my target's left foot by inches. Beckoned on by my other brothers and now thirsty for blood, I threw the second. This one hit, sticking into my brother's left leg. He yelled out in pain, quickly removing the dart as the atmosphere around us shifted from playful to something far more serious. I threw the third dart into my opponent's shin as the onlooking brothers roared. With the look of fear in my youngest brother's eyes now replaced with anger, I rushed to the exit of our makeshift arena, a washing rack lying on its side to prevent our escape. I ran right through it, out of the room and towards my mother's arms, still the only place I felt I truly belonged. But all that was about to change.

As a result of my brother's behaviour, by the age of six I had seen a whole host of weapons from knuckledusters to flick knives and swords, but holding a gun in my hands for the first time is something that will stay with me for ever. I was busy playing with some toys by myself when the door suddenly burst open. It was my eldest brother, who I didn't even know was visiting the house from my nan's where he was then staying. As he walked quietly across the room, the rest of my siblings followed. I watched as they all huddled around in a circle, whispering in excitement. I had no idea what was going on, but I was enchanted as my eldest brother encouraged everyone to come closer. Surrendering the toy in my hand, I headed across the room. As I got closer, I could hear my siblings bickering in low voices: 'Me next. I want to hold it next' . . . 'No, it's my turn.'

Forcing myself into the circle of bodies bigger than my own, I soon realized what all the fuss was about: there was my eldest brother holding a 9-mm handgun. I was instantly struck by its presence. Holding the gun in his left hand, my brother showed us how to remove the magazine with his right. He looked so comfortable as he cocked it back to expose the ejection port, confirming that the chamber was empty. My brother then slid the magazine back into the handle of the gun and it clicked shut. He offered it to my second eldest brother. One by one my brothers passed the gun around as I anxiously awaited my turn. Patiently I stood, my heart hammering against my six-year-old chest. When everybody had finished looking at it, I reached towards the gun, but one of my siblings grabbed for it, desperate to take another look. I raised my voice in protest and my eldest brother interceded, directing my other siblings to let me have a look. The next thing I knew, the gun was in my hands. I remember being surprised by how heavy it was. The gun possessed power and, as young as I was, I could feel it. I could feel its darkness, I could feel its strength. Even then, I knew it wasn't just a gun. It was a machine built for harm and destined to destroy. I had never felt anything like it in my whole short life. I imagined what it would be like to shoot it, not knowing the magnitude of damage that it was capable of. As I held it, I felt a darkness wash over me. I was far too young then to realize how this moment was shaping me.

Though my eldest brother no longer lived with us, he visited regularly, always with a few of his friends in tow. Like my brother, they were ambitious career criminals and though I imagine my parents knew a little of what they were up to, they always welcomed them in. I guess they could relate to how difficult life must be for those young men, but having them around was an undeniable draw for me. When they visited, I would creep out into the garden after dark to join them while they drank and smoked, and if I was lucky, my brother would let me swig whatever he was drinking. Being no older than six or seven years old and swigging beer with my eldest brother and his friends made me feel accepted. I had found my place and knew that if only I could remain there, everything would be all right.

If my brother was involved, I wanted to be involved too – even if I didn't know the full extent of what I was actually getting involved in. Once, while my eldest brother was staying with us, he called me into his bedroom.

'Claud?' he shouted and I instantly came running.

'Go and look for this thing that I've dropped,' he said.

'What is it?' I replied, eager to please him; he was my big brother, my idol.

'It's this large lump of dark plasticine,' he described as I listened intently. 'I dropped it somewhere downstairs. Just go and get it for me.'

With just the minimum information I needed to be useful, I went to look for it. I was so proud that my brother had finally given me a mission of my own. I remember, as I wandered around the house looking at the floor for anything that resembled dark plasticine, the sun shining down through the windows and the feeling of belonging to something or, rather, *someone*. I promised myself that I was going to find this lost item even if it took me all day.

As it happened, it wasn't long before I found the plasticine-type substance and ran as quickly as my seven-year-old legs would carry me to deliver it to my brother. Handing it over to him, I felt an indescribable achievement: I'd completed my mission, I'd actually done it. It wasn't until many years later, when I began drug dealing myself, that I learnt the stuff my brother had sent me to find was a large lump of hashish, a cannabis product of compressed, purified stalk resin.

My brother was such a big part of my early childhood but, sadly, by the time I was seven going on eight, he had been arrested for a violent crime and in the court case that followed, it was decided that he had to go to prison. Back then, I didn't know of anyone who had had a family member go to prison and it knocked me for six. All of a sudden, my difficulty in relating to other children shot into overdrive: how could I possibly relate to those kids who had all their family members at home? How was I meant to keep playing with my toys now that I'd played with a gun? Sadness and shame washed over me. I already felt the world was against me, and having my eldest brother sent to prison was just another example of how dysfunctional my family really was. The darkness began to eat away at me day after day as the feelings of unworthiness inside me grew stronger. As a young boy of not even ten years old, I just didn't know how to manage my feelings.

I remember writing letters to my brother while he was in prison, particularly over Christmas, when I would send him drawings of our Christmas tree. But there were times when we would go to visit him in person. I will never forget the first time I went with my mother to see him. I knew he was doing time at Feltham Young Offenders Institution but, looking back, the building itself feels pretty inconsequential. What I remember most is my mother's face as it came time to say our goodbyes. She watched as my brother wished me well, kissing me on the forehead as I struggled to stop the tears from coming. I quickly turned to walk away, not looking at my brother as I didn't want him to see me crying. It wasn't what men did – but then again, I was only a boy. Bravely, my mother followed me down the corridor, out of sight of my brother before crumbling into tears herself. I will always remember standing there, looking up at her as she hid her face, trying so very hard to control the overwhelming sadness that had come over her as tears poured down my own cheeks like balls rolling down a hill.

Looking back, it's easy to see the warning signs that perhaps following in my eldest brother's footsteps wasn't the best idea – it had landed him behind bars, after all. But to my young impressionable mind it wasn't like the alternatives were much better. When I was just a little bit older, I decided to go to work with my father and brothers as they helped to renovate an old Victorian four-storey building in Streatham

Hill. After unpacking the equipment from the van, we entered the old, derelict building to find every wall on every floor covered in graffiti. It was an intimidating sight and I was soon ordered to go to the back of the pack as we slowly made our way upstairs. When we arrived at the top of the final flight of stairs, I glanced down at the mess of graffiti we had left behind before one of my brothers apprehensively pushed the door in front of us open.

It was like something out of a movie. The door swung open to reveal nothing but darkness. The room was painted completely black, from floor to ceiling, wall to wall. Entering the room, someone noticed a hatch in the centre of the ceiling and soon one of my brothers was standing on a toolbox, opening it and pulling himself up into the loft. He shouted back to us, 'Looks like someone's been sleeping in here.' That wasn't unusual for the jobs my father would be working on, but if we thought what was at the top of the house was bad, we never could have imagined what was underneath.

As my father started working upstairs, he asked two of us to go down to the basement to clear everything out of it – it wasn't a request, it was an expectation. It didn't take long for my brother's dramatic grumbling to start and the more he complained, the more I laughed. As we opened the door to the basement, we heard the scurry of rats running away deeper into the darkness. With every step we descended, we heard more rats move – the place was swarming. Eventually, we began moving boxes, finding more and more rats, both dead and alive, and I've never been able to forget it.

As a result of this and many moments like it, I turned to my father one day and told him that I had no intention of following in his footsteps and doing manual labour when I was grown up. I waited with bated breath, knowing my father had a short fuse for any sort of nonsense. Then he just started laughing, not even bothering to take me seriously. In contrast, I remember turning to my eldest brother and asking him if I could be in his gang when I grew up. 'Sure thing, bro,' he nodded generously, filling me with reassurance. Having spent so many hours listening to my brother tell story after story of his criminal lifestyle by this point, it had become acceptable to me. More than that, it was what I *aspired* to do.

Around the time I was eleven, my mother and eldest brother – who was now out of prison – made some kind of agreement to acquire a greengrocer's on Brixton Hill, between Brixton and Streatham Hill. It was an old, open-fronted place, which meant that it was always cold – and filled with the smell of Chinese food drifting in from the restaurant next door. My mother had dreams of using the shop as a legitimate means of creating income for our family. Sadly, my brother had other ideas.

As my mother and I worked in the shop, we would hear my brother zooming up to the storefront, skidding to a halt outside in whatever vehicle he was driving at the time. Soon he would be approached by some shifty-looking characters who would follow him inside and towards the back of the shop. Reappearing a few minutes later, these visitors would hurry off with whatever it was my brother had just given them. Late into the evening, my brother would use the shop as a place to socialize, smoking cannabis and drinking with his friends. I walked into the shop one morning around

Christmas to find the decorations my mother had so lovingly put up around the place knotted around the ceiling fan after one of my brother's wild parties: it was such a symbol of the vastly different expectations my mother and brother had for the place. Soon these differences would see them parting ways in this venture for good, a fallout between my brother and my father causing the final blow.

I can't really remember what happened exactly. All I know is that my brother was no longer welcome at the shop and, with him gone, my father quickly stepped into his place. Before long, my father had taken over completely, his behaviour totally destroying any last chance my mother had of living out her dreams of being a successful greengrocer. My father started spending more time at the shop and less time at work and, although he had no experience, his controlling nature meant that he would be insistent on every aspect of how the shop should be run.

One day while he was at the shop, he and my mother got into a huge argument, which I could hear coming from the rear of the shop. I went to watch, can of fizzy drink still in my hand, as my father shouted on and on at my mother. Then his eyes locked on me. I turned to walk away, but it was too late, my father lifting his arm to thump me powerfully on the back. Everything seemed to happen in slow motion: the can hitting the floor, my mother screaming, the fizzy drink bleeding across the tiles. On the floor, I silently watched the can roll away as the pain screamed through me.

Then I felt someone shove me in the back, pushing me to stand as I came to my senses. I looked around to see my mother screaming at me to get in the car. With the sound of my father's shouting filling the atmosphere with panic, she grabbed her bag and led me out of the shop, towards her car. We tumbled into each side, and my mother instantly locked it and started the engine. My father followed us, cursing aggressively as we pulled away. I couldn't bring myself to look back.

We drove and drove and drove, neither one of us saying anything. I remember feeling sick to my stomach, somehow accountable for what had happened. I couldn't bring myself to ask her where we were going or what we were going to do. My mother just looked straight ahead as our surroundings grew more and more unfamiliar.

After driving for what felt like hours, she eventually slowed the car, parked and scrambled out. I knew to follow her lead. We made our way to the front door of a flat that I didn't recognize, though I did recognize the lady who answered it. I guess you'd call her a 'family friend', even though I'd only seen her once or twice in my entire life. Soon the lady was nervously inviting us into her small flat and then her living room, where she and my mum exchanged small talk before not too subtly ushering me into the kitchen. She offered me a diluted orange juice before taking a coffee through to my mum and pulling a thin wall divider between us.

I sat there at the small kitchen table for the next couple of hours, pretending that I couldn't hear what my mother and the lady were speaking about. In an attempt to distract myself, I looked round the room, instantly drawn to a small glass paperweight with a scorpion captured inside. Turning the weight over in my hands, I wondered how something with the potential to be so powerful had become so trapped. Were these things destined or was it just a case of being in the wrong place at the wrong time?

It was well into the night before the lady and my mother had seemingly run out of things to talk about. After saying our farewells, we got back into the car. As we drove in the dark, we didn't say much, but I could sense that things hadn't gone as planned. What were we going to do now? If we went home, my mother would almost definitely be on the receiving end of my father's physical abuse.

But where else would we go?

Eventually, after driving for some time, I recognized that we were back in familiar territory. By the time we arrived in Tooting, it was the early hours of the morning, everything was closed and the usual hustle and bustle had died completely. As we drove along the streets, I looked out of the car window into the darkness and felt that familiar feeling of unworthiness washing over me, the black cloud of self-doubt and hatred increasing inside me. Arriving at our destination, a darkness had filled the car too as my mother parked it and switched off the engine. She turned to give me a reassuring smile as she suggested I climb into the back seat to sleep. As I lay there, my mother opened her window about an inch before lighting a cigarette and I slowly fell asleep looking up at the warm yellow glow of an old street lamp.

My mother was already awake when I woke up early the next morning; I doubt she got any sleep. I looked around to see we were in Tooting Common car park, and I was reassured somehow to simply see the light of day.

'Are you OK?' she asked me, forcing a smile.

I nodded as she turned her key in the ignition and we set off again. This time I knew we were heading for my nan's. On our way, we stopped off at a shop, so my mother could buy some more cigarettes, and my eyes couldn't help but catch on a large black-and-white Formula 1-type toy car on the shelves. Quietly, my mother asked if I wanted it and I nodded. It was our usual routine, the best way she knew to show me her love.

We drove around for a little while longer before arriving at my nan's one-bedroom flat in Brixton, just behind the prison. I sat on the kitchen floor and played with my new toy car as my mother explained to my nan everything that had happened. When night-time came, my mother settled down to sleep on the settee, while I slept on two armchairs pushed together. We repeated this routine for a few more nights, me never knowing when it might end. During our stay, one of my brothers came to visit us. He talked to my mother for a long time until eventually she got upset. After about a week of staying there, my mother decided it was time to go back home, my father's behaviour be damned.

In many ways, I felt safer at my nan's, sitting on her kitchen floor, playing with my new toy, but even in my young mind I knew that it couldn't last for ever. We needed clothing and other provisions; we simply had nowhere else to go.

According to figures from the Office for National Statistics, there is a proven link between poverty and domestic abuse. Statistics on violent crime in England and Wales show that women living in the poorest households are more than three times more likely to be victims of domestic abuse than those in higher-income families. The United Nations and many other leading organizations seeking to tackle cycles of poverty have also identified a link between poverty and education. Access to high-quality primary education, and the skills and stability this offers, means that people are able to access higher education and better-paid jobs. The problem, however, is that poverty is also the very thing that makes securing a good education so hard.

And I was about to find out just some of the countless reasons why.

THAT WAS THE DAY I
LEARNT ONE OF THE
GREATEST LESSONS
OF MY LIFE: WITH FEAR
COMES RESPECT.

CHAPTER THREE

Looking out of the top-floor window of the boys' toilets, I savoured the city landscape as it stretched on for miles. The grey tones of the buildings against the bold blue sky reminded me of oil paints, mixed effortlessly and marked with lines made by the cranes that stood tall against a sea of city buildings. I used to tell my teachers that I needed the bathroom just to go and look at that view. It was the only thing I liked about school, the only place I felt peace.

I was not what you would consider academically gifted so, for me, school was a struggle from start to finish. For the most part I spent my days finding reasons not to go. As a relatively poor family, nursery just wasn't something we did, so my academic education began at the age of five. Penwortham Primary was about a 15-minute walk from where we lived in Tooting. It was a large mixed-gender school with around 600 children, and after spending every day with my mother, I found the transition extremely difficult. One day I was at home playing with toys, my mother by my side; the next I was thrust into a classroom of strangers, with no social skills with which to relate to them.

To make matters worse, my first teacher, Mrs Thomas, had a cold approach to teaching. She would set us tasks and then leave us to do them on our own. The rule was simple: once we'd finished our work, we could go and sit on the carpet for story time. While other children who had been to nursery or had started reading and writing with their

29

parents at home cracked on with the task, I would find myself sitting there with absolutely zero understanding of what was required of me. Sometimes the other children would try to help, but ultimately I was left sitting at the desk on my own, crying from the humiliation as Mrs Thomas continued to read to the other children sitting quietly and cross-legged on the carpet. The message was simple: I was inadequate, unworthy and I felt dejected.

Mrs Thomas would sometimes let me join in the carpet time for the last ten minutes, but by then the damage was done. All the other children would watch as I made my way over to them, the embarrassment unbearable as I sat there trying to control the disturbance of my hiccups due to my crying. I would sit, the anxiety and doubt eating away at me as the story went on. This routine continued every day and I wanted to avoid it at all costs.

I started skipping school, pretending to be sick, begging my mother not to make me go – and a lot of the time she didn't make me. I remember one occasion when I was about six, a welfare officer came to visit our home because I had taken so much time off school. As I watched her approach from an upstairs window, I saw her catching some of my siblings playing outside. Knowing that she would soon be in the house, I ran into my mother's bedroom and pretended to be asleep on her bed. As the officer walked into the room, she took one look at me and agreed that I looked unwell.

On the days I did go to school, I was beginning to get a reputation for fighting. It wasn't that I was a particularly bad child, but as a shy, overweight kid who had no idea how to relate to others, I occasionally fell victim to bullying. I was too embarrassed to ever tell anybody, so I resorted to the only other way I knew to deal with opposition: violence.

It was at the time when my brother was really into fitness and martial arts so, after school, he would secretly take me into our room and teach me how to block and punch. It wasn't long before the inevitable happened. The school bully found me in the playground and started to tease me about my weight, my family, my mother. I could feel my blood boil inside me as he spoke – the months and months of ridicule and abuse having built up inside me. Then I lost it. With all my strength I pushed him against a wall. He swung a punch at me but, as my brother had taught me, I raised my left arm to block the blow. I then grabbed the kid and began to punch and punch. As I hit him time and time again across the face and around the back of the head, he wriggled like a snake caught in a trap. I just carried on regardless. By the time the kid managed to escape, I had hit him so many times, my right hand had gone numb. That was the day I learnt one of the greatest lessons of my life: with fear comes respect.

When we truly fear something, we also respect it because we know just how powerfully great it really is. Some people struggle when the Bible talks about the 'fear of God', because if God is love, why should we be afraid? But this kind of fear is more like awe. However, I was a few years away from discovering what that really meant. Back then, putting fear into the minds of others was the only way I knew – the only way I had been taught – to gain control. Looking back, I can now understand that people often put others down in order to make themselves feel better, because they cannot handle the reality of their own life. In the same way that my brother taught me how to block, fighting itself was a means of blocking out what was really going on inside me.

I had never really felt safe or comfortable anywhere, but being in school soon went from bad to worse. If primary school was tough, I was in for a rude awakening at Graveney Secondary School, which had around 2,000 mixed-gender students. There were so many people from so many backgrounds, and my lack of social and academic skills meant that going there quickly became unbearable. So many of these reasons – from being bullied for my family background, to not knowing how to act – found their root in my family's poor economic background. For example, even though our uniform consisted of nothing more than a white shirt and black trousers, mine was never good enough. I always used to wear trainers and my mother would constantly be writing notes to explain why I didn't have the right kind of shoes: finding my size was difficult and when we did, they would wear out quicker than we could afford to replace them; it's the same reason I never had any school books. In recent years the National Education Union has found that the poverty gap between students is getting bigger, with one teacher in its survey (2019) claiming: 'The number of students displaying difficult behaviours has increased and poverty is most certainly a factor.' One of the practical ways my family's lack of wealth was reflected in my life was the sheer number of times we had to move house.

As a child, I wasn't fully aware of just how much my parents were struggling to cope financially and though my mother did all she could, soon my parents were falling behind on mortgage payments, which left us with no choice but to give up the home we were living in, in Pollards Hill. I remember my mother ringing the wealthy property developer my father had worked for six days a week since before I was born in a last desperate attempt to get help. She cried and pleaded, but the developer wouldn't budge. Eventually, he called her back and made her an offer: we could go to a two-bedroom cottage in a place called Surbiton, but if we wanted it, we had to go *now*.

In just one night, we packed every single thing in our ten-room house, our attic and our garage, including me and two of my brothers, my sister, her abusive boyfriend, two three-piece suites, two dogs and a cat. We worked through the night to make trips back and forth from our old home to Surbiton. It was dark when we first arrived, but I could tell the cottage was tiny. Our things quickly filled the attic, and the rest had to be stored in the small living room. As this was the room the front door opened into, we had to use the side entrance to get into the house instead. My parents slept in the double room, my sister slept in the second bedroom, which was also used as an office, my brothers slept on the floor in the living room, and I slept on the floor under the stairs. Each time someone walked up or down them, dust would fall on the area where I slept – but at least I didn't have to roll up the covers and make my own bed every night like my brothers.

Adjusting to life in Surbiton was a culture shock, and one that I didn't handle well. Surrey life was miles away from what I knew and, to make matters worse, for the first year we lived there, I still went to school in Tooting, which meant that my parents had to drive me every day. Due to my parents' work, we had to get up really early and I remember arriving at school before the teachers and having to wait around for the canteen to open at 7 a.m. I would always be tired in class, which coupled with everything else just made it even harder to learn. I was in the bottom class for all of my subjects. In fact, the only time I made it into a top class was when my own teacher threw me out of the lesson and I had to sit in the head of year's class so that she could keep an eye on me. Every lesson, she sat me at the front of the class at a single fold-out table, gave me an old worksheet and told me to get on with it. The first time I walked into that class everybody laughed and asked what I was doing there. Word spread about me getting thrown out of class and soon the other teachers seemed to target me too. I still remember the last words my geography teacher said to me as he threw me out of his class: 'Go and sit in the corridor on your own, like the cockroach you are.'

Uninterested in schoolwork and unaccepted by my peers, I continued to act out and seek attention through bullying and fighting. And it wasn't just my teachers' and classmates' attention I was after; fighting was still the only way to get my father's attention, the only thing that would get him interested enough to tell me off, so I did it more and more. Even the very few friends I managed to make didn't know where they stood with me.

There was one particular incident where a friend of mine who had learning difficulties asked me if he could tell me a funny joke, but warned me beforehand that it was a joke about people's mothers and he didn't want to insult me or mine. I said that it was OK, but once he had told the joke, I flipped, suddenly telling him that as soon as we left the classroom I was going to beat him up. As I made my way to the playground to follow through with the threat, I truthfully didn't want to – he was my friend and he was only joking – but I felt that I had to, otherwise I'd lose any credibility I had managed to build. I had recently watched my brother knock a guy clean out, and wanting to look as hard as I could, I hit him. I remember feeling disappointed that he didn't go down, so I hit him again. I left him slumped and whimpering against the bannisters of the dark staircase and went out to the playground to tell my other friends, but they weren't bothered. Looking back, they were probably growing up, getting bored with my fighting, but I just didn't know how to stop.

The bell rang and students soon began streaming from the playground to line up outside our classroom. That's when I saw the kid I had just attacked. In a weak attempt to intimidate him further, I began acting like a fool with a friend of mine, pretending that I wasn't fazed by my totally unprovoked attack earlier. He tried his best not to look bothered, but this only infuriated me and so, with everyone watching, I hit him in the back of the head again and again until he began to cry. I turned to look at my friends, thinking they would praise me, but they didn't; everyone just stood watching silently until a girl I'd also recently bullied stepped forward to put her hand on the kid's back. 'Are you all right?' I heard her ask quietly, before escorting him away. Soon after, our teacher arrived and we all entered the classroom, but just as we sat down the headmaster stormed in.

'Outside, now!' He pointed directly at me as the others fell into stunned silence.

Reluctantly, I followed him to his office. He sat, red in the face, as I tried to explain away my stupid behaviour, but I knew it was too late.

'I've had enough,' he sighed. 'If you get into any more trouble, you will be expelled for good,' he explained. 'So it might just be better if you take it upon yourself to leave.'

Even in the moment, I knew that he had a point. When I was at school, I was disruptive, fighting or talking back in class. More often than not I wasn't there at all. Then there were other times, the *worst* times, when my father would barge into the school of his own accord and demand that I leave the classroom immediately, shouting down the teacher and embarrassing me in front of everybody. No matter what I did, I couldn't fit in anywhere. I wasn't smart enough for the smart kids. I wasn't bad enough for the bad kids, because even then my father would somehow end up stealing the limelight. Deep in my core, I just knew that I wasn't good enough. I had followed my brother's advice about defending myself, but in the process I had grown into nothing more than a spiteful, screwed-up bully.

I stayed at home for a number of months before joining a new school in Surbiton. I was still only 12 at the time, but by then I already hated the person I had become and vowed that this new school would be my fresh new start. Sadly, like so many things in my life that far, things didn't go according to plan. Though fighting was now normal to me, I was about to encounter a reason for it that I hadn't come across until then: racism.

My new school had a capacity of around 700 students, yet it only had two black students and one mixed-race student there: *me*. Racism was rife, from the racial slurs written on the toilet walls to the use of racist terms like 'nigger' and 'coon' in the classroom. The teachers there would simply turn a blind eye. From my first day at the start of the second year, I became aware of a child from Korea who would get beaten up daily by bullies and an older gang of guys who sometimes surrounded him on the way home from school. By the beginning of the third year, this poor kid had left the school. Once again, I found myself feeling extremely vulnerable, insecure and uncomfortably aware that I didn't belong there. But this time it wasn't because of the clothes I wore or the music I listened to; it was because of the colour of my skin. It was the first time in my life that I became aware of my mixed-race heritage and, as a result, I began to feel more and more uncomfortable with myself and with those around me.

According to the 'Annual bullying survey 2015' (Ditch the Label), key findings show that appearance is cited as the number one aggressor of bullying, with 51 per cent of individuals who were asked saying that they were bullied because of attitudes towards how they look. And racism is not just rife among students. Runnymede Trust, the UK's leading independent think tank on race equality and race relations, published a report entitled 'Race and racism in English secondary schools' in June 2020. The Trust found that 'racism is deeply embedded in schooling' and 'schooling must be radically reimagined to place a commitment to anti-racism at its core'. It also found that teaching staff in English secondary schools are still 'overwhelmingly white' and 'by their own admission, many teachers are ill prepared to teach in ways that promote anti-racism, and this can include BME teachers'.

By my third year, a little like it was for the student from Korea, school was a nightmare. Ironically, I'd gone from being the bully to being bullied. I never suffered anything more than occasional name-calling and could easily have fought back or told my brothers, but I was so emotionally drained that I just couldn't be bothered. I wanted to be free from all of the dysfunctional violence and aggression that had by now followed me around for years. The dark cloud of negativity that had surrounded me was continuing to grow and I hated my life more than ever before. It was around this time that a friend of mine who lived down the road told me about a youth club at my school run by the local church.

I was hesitant at first, because I wasn't sure who would be there, but part of me wanted to find out. I soon found myself asking my mother if I could go and, somehow, she managed to clear it with my father on two conditions: first, that I was home by the time the streetlights came on and, second, that I stayed with Phil. Phil was in my class at school and throughout the struggle with everything had become my best friend. So, once a week, we walked to the youth club together, where we would play football and get up to harmless mischief – sometimes we *tried* to get up to more, slipping away to explore the parts of school we weren't meant to go in, but it was never long before one of the youth leaders noticed we were gone and brought us back into the group.

I started to really enjoy the Thursday evenings spent there and my mother even ended up extending my curfew and scraping together a couple of pounds so that I could go and get fish and chips with the other guys. But before we left for chips, the leaders would ask us all to gather together in the social area for prayer. We'd all be asked to sit quietly and shut our eyes while one of the leaders gave thanks and, though I didn't always engage, it felt nice just to be a part of something. I had no idea how much that prayer time had come to mean to me until one evening my friend tried to ruin it.

I remember how, as we closed our eyes to pray, a friend of mine started to whistle. Everyone opened their eyes, fixing them directly on me. Not knowing what else to do, I shrugged my shoulders and the youth leader calmly requested that we all close our eyes again to pray. After prayer, the same leader came over to ask me if I was the one who had been whistling. I told him it wasn't me, but refused to tell him who it was, even though, for some reason, I knew my friend had gone too far in trying to ruin our prayers. I wanted to tell the truth, but with all my friends looking at me and my self-worth still next to nothing, I couldn't.

When we left the club that night, my friend wouldn't stop laughing about what had happened, but I just couldn't find it funny. That night, as I lay in bed, I couldn't settle; deep down I felt that everything had been spoilt and it was all my fault. As that familiar darkness clouded over me, my mind started to race. I thought about my old school, how it would be easier if I was there, but I couldn't go back because of how I'd behaved. I thought about my new school and why I didn't fit in. I thought about my father hitting my mother, about the cold black gun that my eldest brother had brought to our house, about the drugs I had found for him and the praise he had rewarded me with. A million thoughts ran through my mind over and over again until eventually I fell asleep. I had no idea then that I had encountered something of Jesus and was about to discover more.

I went to youth club consistently for about a year and, though my school attendance was dwindling, on one rare occasion, I found myself happy to be there. As the entire school gathered together for assembly, I was taken by surprise to see the youth leader from our club sitting next to a slightly older, scruffy-looking man on the stage. The chap had long, reddish, greasy hair and tattoos going down both arms. He was wearing a grey T-shirt and a washed-out pair of jeans with some black boots; he looked like he knew how to fight.

As the headteacher stood up to introduce our guest, the whole place fell silent and every student waited in anticipation. The man was called Brian Greenaway and he was there to tell us his story. You could have heard a pin drop as Brian took a step towards the front of the stage and began to tell us how he had once been the president of a Hell's Angels chapter. He spoke about how he'd been severely violent and full of hate, and how one day he had a godly experience that changed his life. I was taken back by just how dysfunctional Brian's life had been, but as he spoke I was filled with hope, a kind of hope that I hadn't felt before.

I don't remember how long the assembly lasted, but as it drew near to the end, Brian said something about how God could change our lives too – all we had to do was ask. He then encouraged everyone who wanted to, to do just that.

I don't recall exactly what I prayed for as we were sitting there in silence, but I know that in my heart I meant it. I was tired of the life that I had been living and was ready for change. I didn't want the assembly to end and as all the students were being ushered out of the hall, my youth leader caught my eye. He greeted me with a smile and said that he had something to give me. I looked down and he reached out and handed me a book based on Brian's life, called *Hell's Angel*. I quickly stuffed it into my school bag before any of the other kids noticed and, as soon as school was over, I began to read it. As I read his story, the hope in me was at an all-time high. I was fully charged and couldn't wait for the next youth club session so that I could see the leader; I had something that I needed to ask him.

Thursday couldn't come quickly enough as I counted down the days to youth club. Finally, the day came and then the moment when my friends knocked for me and I ran to get my coat and make my way to the school, trying my best to contain my secret excitement. When we arrived, I looked around for Richard, the youth leader, but he wasn't anywhere to be seen, so we headed towards the sports hall where we would usually play football. As we entered the hall, I saw him refereeing a match and instantly felt the excitement charging through my body. We sat around the outside of the pitch while the other matches took place, then finally it was our turn and Richard asked if we were ready. My friends wanted to play so badly, but all I could think about was how I was going to get the opportunity to speak to him. Finally, when he suggested we all stop for a break, I knew this was my chance.

'Richard!' I shouted behind him as we walked away from the sports hall. He turned to look at me. 'I been reading that Brian Greenaway book that you gave me,' I began nervously.

'Oh yeah? What do you think of it?' Richard replied.

'I've got a copy too,' Phil interrupted beside me; Phil always followed where I went.

'It's really good,' I said, ignoring Phil and speeding up to walk beside Richard. 'In fact, I've been wondering . . .' I could feel my heart hammering in my chest. 'Do you think you could get me a Bible?'

Richard stopped in his tracks on the staircase. 'You want a Bible?' he said, turning to look me in the eye. Phil was staring at me too.

'Yeah, I do,' I replied, my mouth dry.

'Are you absolutely *sure* you want a Bible?' Richard asked again, clearly thinking I was up to no good. I kind of wanted Phil to think that too and smirked a little while I nodded. 'OK.' Richard looked at me, unsure. 'I'll sort it out and get back to you.'

I turned to head back down to the football hall in great satisfaction – Phil following behind. I thought that Richard was going to get back to me at some point that evening, but he didn't and although I was a little disappointed, I presumed that he just needed some more time to sort it out. I expected that he would get back to me the next week, so I soon began counting down the days. Every day that passed, I read a bit more of Brian's story; I wasn't a confident reader and it was my first attempt at reading a proper book. I found it difficult to stay focused but decided that I was going to continue to try. It was all I could think about. I'd spend my days at school counting down the hours just so I could get home and read, and as the days came and went, I got more and more excited about getting my hands on a Bible.

Thursday evening finally rolled around and I walked to youth club, roaring with hope. I had spent the whole week wondering how Richard would give me my Bible. Would he call me over and discreetly give it to me? What would he say? Would he even say anything at all?

When we finally arrived, Phil and I made our way to the football hall to find Richard already refereeing the matches as usual. We played our usual number of games before taking our usual break, but Richard's behaviour wasn't usual at all. I thought that maybe he was waiting for the youth club to end so that he could give me my Bible in private.

That evening we closed in prayer as we usually did, and I waited around for as long as I possibly could for Richard to call me over, but he never did. The same thing happened the following week, and the week after that and the week after that. I told myself again and again that Richard had just forgotten to get me one or maybe the small church that he belonged to had run out of Bibles and he was too embarrassed to tell me. But I knew I was lying to myself. Once again, I was mad at myself for putting my trust in someone just to get my feelings hurt, for letting another adult fool me into thinking they cared.

I never ever found out what had happened to that Bible, but I knew something was stirring inside me as yet more disappointment left a bitter aftertaste in my heart.

I WAS LOOKING FOR A ROLE MODEL, AND BETWEEN MY ABUSIVE FATHER AND MY ABSENT BROTHERS, I WAS LACKING ONE. THAT WAS UNTIL I FOUND A NEW ROLE MODEL TO SET MY HOPES ON.

CHAPTER FOUR

The weeks passed and Richard still hadn't mentioned the Bible. I told myself I didn't care, but deep down that feeling of rejection took root and any new-found hope I had experienced in Brian Greenaway's talk quickly began to fade. Looking back, I understand that everyone forgets things, everyone makes mistakes – or maybe Richard thought I actually *was* joking about wanting a Bible – but at the time, I didn't have the skill set to handle my perceived rejection sensibly, and as a result his 'broken promise' broke *me*. I quickly stopped persevering with Brian's book – my first proper book – and sooner or later stopped going to youth group all together.

One evening, myself, Phil, Dennis and a couple of local kids were all hanging out together when Den got word that the leader from the youth club was having a meeting inside the local church. He thought it would be a good idea if we all went up to the church and banged on the stained-glass windows where the meeting was taking place. We soon found ourselves doing exactly that, but as the knocks turned to bangs and then thumps, Den's hand smashed straight through the window. Panicked, we all ran away from the church and across the neighbouring fields to seek refuge. As soon as we stopped, Den started to worry; he hadn't meant to do it and he was so scared of getting into trouble. He ran home to lie low.

Shortly after Den left, we saw the church leader walking down the road towards us. I was worried that he would go to my house and tell my parents, so I decided to come into the open to gain his attention and distract him from his destination. As he approached me, I tried to look smug, but the church leader wasn't annoyed. The only one who was annoyed was me; I had so wanted the *youth* leader to follow us. Patiently, the church leader asked me if I had broken the glass. I shook my head as he proceeded to ask who *had* broken it, saying that he would let the incident slide so long as the person who did it paid for the repairs. I later heard that he found Den, who confessed and paid for it. I was just glad my father didn't find out I was involved, as then I would have had to pay for it in more ways than one.

My father continued being violent throughout this time, constantly arguing with my mother. All of my brothers had moved out by now, so once my father started seeing red, there was nothing I could do except stand in between my parents and plead for him not to hit my mother. One evening, I arrived home to hear my parents arguing aggressively from their bedroom. I raced up the stairs as fast as I could and grabbed their bedroom door handle, preparing to burst in and intercept the fight as I had done a million times before – but this time it didn't open. As I heard my mother's screams, I began to shout through the door for my father to stop, but it was useless; *I* was useless. All I could do was wait for the break in my mother's screams every time he hit her, until I couldn't take it any more. Fleeing to my bedroom, I locked the door behind me and put my fingers in my ears, the way I used to do when I was little. By now, the noise wasn't just coming from outside, though. Inside, my anxiety and hopelessness were out of control, a constant hum of dread rushing through my veins.

Eventually the thumps from my parents' room stopped, my mother's screams falling into the silent night, leaving nothing but the sound of her uncontrollable sobbing. I sat on the edge of my own bed, trying my best not to vomit or lose control, knowing an anxiety attack would only anger my father further. Things at home were so bad that I needed an escape, but by now I knew my education wasn't going to be it.

Exam season was fast approaching, but I had no blueprint for what good grades could lead to; none of my family members had ever done anything positive or productive based on the results of their GCSEs. I found the whole thing pretty pointless. With no coursework to show, I was only allowed to sit three exams, and even then I was so uninterested in school – and the school was so uninterested in me – that I answered the questions by ticking random boxes. School was almost done, but my problems at home were far from over, so I spent every opportunity I could hanging around outside with my friends. Looking back, I think that's why youth club had meant so much to me – it was a place to escape – and why the leader's words had given me so much hope and caused me so much hurt. I was looking for a role model, and between my abusive father and my absent brothers, I was lacking one. That was until I found a new role model to set my hopes on.

I can't remember the first time I watched Eric Cantona play football, but it's fair to say he made an impression on me. To many he will be remembered for his technical skill and goal-scoring ability, for being part of Manchester United's 1990s revival, but to me he meant so much more; he was an inspiration. He was a man who stood on his own two feet and wasn't afraid of anything; outlawed by many but a leader to others. He carried around a poor disciplinary record for most of his career, and I related to his outbursts of emotion. In 1995, when he got convicted for fly kicking a fan, he successfully appealed against his two-week prison sentence and I remember watching the press conference that followed. The media and paparazzi assembled in their masses to take photos and ask question after question, but as Cantona calmly sipped his water a silence fell across the crowd, and then he spoke: 'When seagulls follow the trawler, it is because they think sardines will be thrown into the sea.' Then, without breaking his cool exterior, he thanked everyone and left the room, leaving everyone stunned. He was bold and brave, and I wanted to be like him.

Before long, football became my everything. My mother, still trying her best to buy me everything I wanted, bought me countless Manchester United football kits, all with Cantona's name and number printed on the back of the shirts. I'd always have a kit on and would spend every moment I could outside of the house with a football by my feet. Sometimes I would stand in the middle of the quiet road in front of our house and practise doing keep-ups for hours. My mother even bought me a piece of equipment that helped me practise my kicking accuracy – it had a handle with an extension lead on it that you attached the football to so that when you kicked the football it would extend about twenty yards and then come bouncing back for you to repeat the kick.

Thankfully, Phil was also into football and we would spend countless hours over the summer watching any games we could and then rushing out to dive through the hole in the fence and on to the school fields to try our best to re-enact the goals we had all seen scored on television earlier that day. I played football any time I could. I played at school during lunch and then again after school, and on the days I didn't go to school, I played all day; I even played in the rain. Though I played and played, by 13 years old I was over 6 feet tall and weighed 13 stone, so I soon learnt that I had a better chance of keeping up with the others by playing in goal.

I loved being a goalkeeper and was so excited by the burden of expectation spectators place on players in this position. I studied the likes of David Seaman and Peter Schmeichel, and though I didn't have the speed and agility to make a brilliant footballer, I like to think I became a fairly good goalkeeper; I even started playing for a local team. The football team consisted of a bunch of lads who were so different from the people I was used to. They were loud and confident and they stuck up for one another. Playing in this team started to build my confidence and my mother even managed to get in touch with Wimbledon Football Club and arrange a trial for me.

Soon after my mother told me the time and date of my trial, I decided that I wasn't going to tell anybody about it – in case I jinxed it. Sadly, the 13-year-old me just couldn't contain his excitement and when my eldest brother came to visit us one evening, I couldn't miss the opportunity to impress him. Phil and I were busy playing football on the school fields as usual, when suddenly my brother and a couple of other guys approached us. Phil and the other kids we were with instantly stopped playing and went over to greet my brother and his friends; everybody had something they wanted to tell him, but no more so than me. I picked up the football, put it under my arm and ran over to see him. I was buzzing with excitement and couldn't wait to tell him about my football trials. I stood there waiting and waiting for my opportunity to speak, when finally he asked me what I'd been up to lately. I seized the opportunity, excitedly telling him all about the football I had been playing, before eventually telling him the best bit of all: Mum had managed to arrange trials for me. I looked to my brother, who stood with one hand in his pocket, puffing on a spliff. The silence stretched between us as I anticipated his response, watching his expression go from smiling to frowning before finally responding.

'But why the hell would they choose you?'

I tried my best not to look shocked, but I was totally caught off guard. 'What do you mean?' I asked, clearly confused.

'I *mean*,' he began, ready to drive the point home in front of everyone, 'there are millions of kids that want to play football, so why would they choose *you*? Look at you!'

I watched as my brother smirked, taking another smoke of his spliff. I had nothing to say in response; I felt like such a fool. He was probably right about the trials, but he hadn't even seen me play. He had no idea about my footballing ability. I couldn't actually remember the last time he had seen me full stop. His response was motivated by nothing other than his opinion of me. For the last couple of years football had been my only outlet. I had put everything into it, and yet in just a few short seconds another dream was shattered.

As I stood there in front of him, his words of disdain echoing in my mind, I felt physically sick. Looking down at the football tucked under my arm, the embarrassment I felt was almost unbearable. I was such a fool. How could I ever have thought someone would choose me? That I would ever be good enough? The one person whose opinion I valued more than anybody else's in the entire world had shown me in a few short seconds just how much he valued me. The man I had been trying to impress ever since before I could remember thought I was as worthless as I felt. I was trash; it was time to accept that.

From that moment on, I never played football seriously again. I stopped playing for the local football club, I quit going to training. I stopped wearing my football kits and couldn't bear to even *look* at anything to do with football; I packed away everything football related that I owned. As the time for my Wimbledon Football Club trials finally came, the club sent me a letter to confirm the date and time – I couldn't even look at it. My mother tried to get me to reconsider, to ask why I now despised something I had once loved, but there was nothing she could say that was going to change my mind.

Looking back, I can see that my reaction was about more than just football. I don't know if I ever really expected to be a professional footballer, but at the time I just needed something to hold on to. My childhood had been so difficult up until that point, my schooling so horrific, my home life even worse, that I just needed something to believe in. From putting my hope in that youth leader to falling in love with football, I was searching for freedom, some form of escape. Once again, it hadn't worked. I needed something stronger.

I began smoking cigarettes, and smoking with Phil soon became my favourite thing to do. As soon as I woke up I would get ready, then go and knock for him, and together with some of our friends we would regularly hang out in parks or fields, smoking cigarettes and all chipping in a few quid to buy some beers, even though back then we were still under age. As the biggest of our group it would often fall to me to buy whatever we fancied, but once we'd got our hands on the alcohol we would sit in the field and drink until it got dark. I guess we were just teenagers trying to find our feet in the world, but with all of us feeling forgotten, drinking in a park together felt as good a place as any. That was, until we discovered the garage.

The garage next to our house had always been there, but in the summer of 1998 it began to mean so much more and it soon became the only place we would hang out. It lay at the end of a dirt alleyway that wound all the way down the side and towards the back of our house. Though my parents had previously used it for our car, my brother had since hijacked it as a place he and his mates would chill. They had gas heating, a VHS player, games consoles, a stereo and a microwave – but really we all knew their favourite thing to do in the garage was smoke and drink.

Each day, more and more of my brother's friends would come to lounge around on the old armchairs and sofa inside, trying to find their latest hit. Still in my teens, I used to regularly stay up until the early hours of the morning, hanging out with my brother and his friends while they got drunk, smoked cannabis, snorted cocaine and got high on Ecstasy pills. I stayed away from any hardcore drugs, deeming cigarettes harmless in comparison to what my brother and his friends were experimenting with. I had seen the damage that drugs could do first-hand and was extremely scared of the long-term effects they might have on me. Little did I know then that you didn't have to take drugs to be damaged by them.

I remember a chap called Billy coming to the garage one afternoon to smoke some cannabis. He was about 20 at the time and though he wasn't a regular to the garage, he and my brother had known each other for some time. Shortly after Billy began to roll his spliff, someone else opened a small envelope and emptied some bright white powder on to a small wall tile, one of many tiles scattered across the garage and left readily available to chop and divide cocaine on. After the coke was prepared, the first person would snort it and then pass the tile around until everybody had had some. Eventually the tile came to Billy who, no stranger to cocaine, enthusiastically accepted. I, however, hovered over towards the window, lifting the smoke-stained curtain hung over it to find that the day had drifted into the night. By the time I took my seat back on the sofa, the drugs and drinking session had gained heavy momentum, the Christmas lights hung permanently from the ceiling dancing in and out of the thick cannabis smoke to the beat of the happy hardcore blasting from the stereo.

Before long, a bag of Mitsubishis – Ecstasy pills so called due to having the Mitsubishi car logo neatly engraved into each one – appeared and quickly began to be distributed around the large crowd that had by now congregated within the garage. Billy proceeded to take one, then another, and then another – taking 13 in total – as those around the room cheered him on. I sat back and watched as the crowd inside the garage snorted large amounts of cocaine, drank too much alcohol and popped way too many pills, until my cannabis-heavy eyes grew tired and I decided to go to bed.

I woke up at midday, shortly before my father returned home from work, and spent the rest of the afternoon waking up and getting ready, until around 5 p.m. when my brother and I finally decided to venture into the garage. I followed behind as he opened the door and switched the light on, only to reveal Billy sitting bolt upright asleep on the sofa. We tried to wake him, but he wasn't responsive, so my brother decided the best thing we could do was let him sleep it off. We began clearing up, collecting beer cans, emptying ashtrays, until out of the corner of my eye I saw Billy's body begin to shudder.

I fearfully turned to my brother, whose eyes were fixed on Billy: pale white and sweating profusely. My brother asked him if he was all right, but he just stared back for a few seconds before slumping back on the sofa and immediately going back to sleep. By now people had started to arrive at the garage and were just as surprised as we had been to find Billy still there, sweating through his trip. Every so often

Billy would wake up, his distorted face frantically looking around at everyone before shouting out something random and immediately falling back to sleep. It took Billy three whole days to sober up.

I have no idea what his family thought when he finally arrived home, drenched in sweat and having not eaten in days; his phone had been ringing non-stop until it ran out of battery on that first night. They must have been so worried, but it's not as if we could have answered the phone to his mother and told her that her 20-year-old son was lying in a garage in Surbiton in a drug-induced coma because he had taken 13 pills. I have seen a lot of foul things happen to people while on drugs, but what happened to Billy will always stay with me. I was sure he was about to die and when my brother turned to me the night Billy finally went home, relief in his eyes, I knew he had thought the same.

The garage may have replaced youth club, football, drinking out on the fields, but now that my academic studies were over, the garage became like a new kind of education for me too. My brother wasn't simply taking drugs in our garage, he was selling them. By then I was no stranger to selling goods: soon after I started smoking cigarettes, I was selling them to other kids for 40 pence per cigarette, and at £1.30 for a box of ten, I figured my profit margin wasn't bad. But my brother's activities were on the next level.

I soon learnt that the crowds of so-called friends who came to the garage were nothing but a bunch of drug-addicted customers buying and using on the premises daily. Sitting in the garage at the bottom of our garden, I would watch all sorts of drugs being weighed and bagged, ready for distribution. To anyone else the garage would have been considered a trap house – the place a drug dealer uses to make their profit – but to me it was just normal. Looking back it's hard to see how I ever thought it was, but at the time, after being exposed to so many 'abnormal' patterns of behaviour throughout my childhood, I was starting to lose the will to fight against it; this was my lot, this was what was normal for me.

I WAS SO CONFIDENT THAT THIS WAS THE LIFE-CHANGING OPPORTUNITY THAT I HAD BEEN WAITING FOR, BUT I COULDN'T HAVE BEEN MORE WRONG.

CHAPTER FIVE

During the summer of 1998, day after day spent in the garage soon rolled into one. Before long, I was celebrating my sixteenth birthday, sitting in the garage playing a console game. Naturally, no one was there for the game.

A lot of the regulars would often come to the garage, get high and play games on the consoles until they came down from whatever drug they were taking and started to process all over again, until they ran out of whatever it was they were taking. One day, I was playing on one of the consoles when I heard a random conversation break out between some of the garage's most regular visitors. One of them was saying quite incredulously to another that he'd gone to sign on and the interviewer at the Job Centre had suggested he get down to a local well-known burger outlet.

'They hirin'?' the other asked, as my ears pricked up all the more. I immediately paused the game and looked across to Phil; it was only in the past couple of weeks that I had begun to talk to him about trying to get a job. School had rejected me, I had rejected football and yet still there was something in me that wanted to prove I wasn't a total failure. I turned my attention back to the guy who was waffling on. Brazenly interrupting, I asked him to confirm that the fast food restaurant was actually recruiting. He nodded in return and then began to tell me his whole pointless Job Centre story all over again; I didn't wait around for him to finish. While he was still talking, I put down the controller and headed for the exit.

'Hey! Where are you going?' my brother called behind me.

'To get a job,' I said defiantly, as the weed-head – who had only just realized I wasn't listening to his story – suggested that I go for it. I thanked him and walked out of the garage. I *really* wanted out of that garage.

Storming straight to the bus stop at the top of our road, I caught the first number 71 that came along. As I sat on the bus, I gazed out of the window, the streets blurring past me as memories raced through my mind. I thought about my past and everything negative that had happened, my father's violence, my brothers' influence, my failed education. Then I thought about my future. Though I felt beaten down by so many circumstances, I still wanted to prove to myself that I had value as a human being. Watching the streets of Surbiton fly by, my mind filled with possibilities. Things were going to change. This job was just the start.

Before I knew it, I was standing in front of the fast food place. I nervously walked up to the counter and asked if there were any job vacancies and if so, could I please get an application.

The young assistant behind the till met me with a smile. 'Sure,' she said. 'Take a seat and I'll bring one over to you.'

She offered me a free drink to have while I waited, and her friendly approach helped to ease my nerves. I waited a few moments before being approached by a lady in a suit, holding an application form in her hand. She sat down next to me and introduced herself as the manager before going over the application with me.

'You do have a National Insurance number?' she asked.

'I do,' I began slowly. How was I supposed to know I needed my National Insurance number? 'But I don't have it with me now. I'll bring it in soon.'

After reading through the rushed application form and asking me a couple of questions, she stood up and congratulated me: she was offering me a job! I left that place absolutely buzzing. It was the first bit of good news I had received in a long time. I couldn't believe that somebody had actually seen something of worth in me and decided to invest in it. It was the best birthday present I could have asked for and I rushed back home to tell the guys in the garage. Looking around the smoke-filled space, I knew my job was my ticket out of there. I was so confident that this was the life-changing opportunity that I had been waiting for, but I couldn't have been more wrong.

My first shift began *very* early and I was tasked with helping to open the restaurant. It began so early, in fact, that there weren't even any buses running at that time. Standing at the bus stop, my anxiety started to rise. What should I do? I couldn't be late. I had so much riding on this opportunity. After a few more minutes of just praying that a rogue number 71 would rock up, I decided my only option was to walk to work – and *quickly*. I headed up the road on the three-mile trip towards Surbiton High Street, wearing too-tight leather shoes that pinched at my heels with every step I took. By the time I finally arrived, my feet were burning. And though I managed to reach the restaurant just in time to start my shift, the manager was waiting at the entrance and wasn't all that happy to see me.

As soon as we were into the restaurant, she sent me straight to the big industrial freezer to fetch stock. I struggled to find exactly what it was she had sent me to look for and began to get frustrated. It was the first time I had ever even been into a freezer. It was absolutely massive, everything was in boxes and yet there was this expectation that it should be simple enough. I struggled to work out what she was after, becoming more and more frustrated, but I refused to fail this seemingly simple task.

After a while, the manager came into the freezer to ask me what was taking so long. Once out of the freezer, she asked me to start frying breakfasts. I was given one opportunity to watch her do it and then it was over to me. I tried my best, but at just 16 and with very little experience other than working in my father's volatile company, I was just not cut out for the fast pace of fast food. In hindsight, I can understand that all I needed was for someone to go slower with me, take the time to understand my background and my experience. At the time, however, I just felt this was one more thing I couldn't do.

Around lunchtime, a new shift began – with a whole host of new employees. Just like the manager who had greeted me, these staff members weren't very sociable or helpful. I remember there was one guy in particular who I felt had decided to make my life a living hell straight from the get-go; he was determined to make everything I did as difficult as possible. He would take trays of my food out of the ovens while they were still cooking and put them on the floor, or take my burgers off the grill and replace them with his. He called me useless at any opportunity, which quickly took its toll on me. Looking back now, this guy was probably just a very unhappy person, but by this point I didn't need anyone to tell me what I already felt: *you're useless, you're a waste of space*. I couldn't be sure what motivated his dislike of me, whether it was my height, my race or something else completely, but it was clear that this man thought I was somehow socially 'below' him, and he targeted me for that. His negative attitude towards me persisted, and within a few days of this new job, I was dreading going to work.

Verbal abuse like this is never easy to deal with, and as I now know today, it is never OK. For me, it reminded me of the abuse I'd suffered at the hands of my dad, my brothers and those at school, and everything within me wanted to slam his head on to the burger grill. And yet this time I didn't have the strength to fight. After years of fighting back and it not getting me anywhere, and with no idea of how to address the situation without violence, I didn't say anything at all. I stayed silent for about two torturous weeks until I couldn't take his verbal abuse any more. Reluctantly I admitted defeat and packed the job in. I also admitted what I already knew: I was useless. There was only one place I belonged. With a heavy heart, I headed back to the garage.

It had been over a fortnight, but things in the garage hadn't changed one bit. The only thing that had really changed was Phil. As my best mate, Phil was a frequent visitor to the garage, but in my absence he had started visiting independently. He'd also begun smoking cannabis and doing cocaine. I was a little disappointed when I first found out that Phil had started doing drugs but, in all honesty, I wasn't really surprised. For as long as I'd known him, Phil couldn't wait to start doing drugs, and in want of any better opportunities, he seized his chance to start using. I remember once when we were younger, he snorted lines of food seasoning off the breakfast table in his kitchen. He loved hanging around with me and my brothers, and often said that he felt more accepted by my family than he did his own. He felt like an outcast and would do pretty much anything in order to fit in. And in *this* family, the family we had found in the garage, drugs were the key to belonging.

With any community a sense of belonging usually begins with an invitation, and it was Phil who invited me to smoke my first spliff. I remember we were sitting in the garage one evening waiting for my brother, Phil smoking a spliff, me smoking a cigarette.

'Go on – have some of this,' he said, turning his nose up at my hit of choice.

'No,' I said. It wasn't the first time I had refused the offer of drugs.

'It's just like smoking a cigarette,' he argued as I refused again. 'Why not?'

Why not? Two simple little words. I had tried to avoid the garage, managed to get myself a job, yet still ended up right back where I started. I felt a far cry away from that little boy who had been excited to get hold of a Bible. Whatever was stirring inside me then had well and truly been snuffed out, and it was time to light up something else. What had I got to lose? Here was Phil, my best friend in the world, offering me something to get through the struggle. *If you can't beat them, join them . . .*

'Sure,' I smiled, finally surrendering and taking the spliff. Phil looked on silently as I put it to my lips and began to smoke. Exhaling, I watched the thick potent cannabis smoke glide away gently through the air, then took another pull; it was so quiet in the garage you could hear the cigarette paper sizzling under the pressure off each toke. I looked back across at Phil and he burst into a fit of laughter. In between giggling, Phil kept asking me what it felt like, his eyes filled with excitement. I gave the spliff back to Phil. I hadn't felt anything.

I didn't know then that this first smoke would pave the way to an excessive use of cannabis, which I smoked daily for around 13 years. Even today I still feel the effects of this, as I struggle to remember things. Research has suggested that smoking marijuana daily may affect short-term memory and that even casual use can lead to brain changes. Another study shows that teenagers who smoke regularly for a number of years but then kick the habit may also see their long-term memory take a hit. At the time, I didn't care.

No sooner had I finished smoking the spliff with Phil than my brother returned from reloading on supplies. Shortly after entering the garage, he opened a massive black plastic bag revealing a large amount of skunk and asked if everybody wanted to roll up, as he usually would. I could see that Phil was itching to tell my brother about what had taken place while he was gone, so I decided to get to him first. As everybody dipped their hands into the cannabis-filled bag, I sat forward on my seat and asked if I could roll up too. My brother refused and I remember feeling confused by his public rejection. It seemed hypocritical of him; all of a sudden he had moral standards?

I wasn't sure if he wasn't allowing me to roll up because he loved me and wanted the best for me, or simply because he didn't want to share his cannabis with me, even though he shared it with everyone else. Was I not even good enough to be a drug user? Yet again, I was being cast out, but this time I was being cast out even by the outcasts. Phil ticked a draw (giving me drugs now for payment later) and allowed me to roll up. I was once again wounded by my brother's words, which only goaded me to smoke.

Later on that evening my eldest brother came to visit and he and my other brother stepped outside of the garage for a discussion. I couldn't hear what was being said, but I could tell that they were talking about me. Shortly afterwards my brother came back into the garage and said that I had to go outside to speak with my eldest brother. I was initially hesitant, as I wasn't sure why he would want to talk to me, or what about. I thought that he might tell me off for smoking, but I was just happy to get some personal time with him, so took the opportunity. He still carried that reputation – the one everyone wanted to be with – and as his littlest brother, I was far from immune to his charm.

When I got outside, my eldest brother invited me to sit with him in his car. Trying not to show my inner enthusiasm, I walked slowly over to the passenger seat door, opened it and got in. It was slightly awkward; there was definitely an elephant in the room, even if I couldn't work out what the hell it was.

'Is it true?' my eldest brother started, as my heart beat faster in my chest. 'Is it true that you've started smoking cannabis?'

I quietly confirmed that it was true and waited for his condemning response. It never came. Instead, after a second that seemed to stretch for a minute, he smiled in response. Sitting back in his seat, he took a deep breath and reached into the pocket of his jacket, pulling out what appeared to be a small rolled-up see-through plastic bag, the type that you put fruit in at a supermarket. As he began to unroll the bag, I noticed that it contained a fair amount of skunk. He opened the bag up and took out what I roughly estimated to be around half of the original amount and told me to hold out my hands. He then filled my palms with the fluffy light green skunk buds and told me to enjoy my first proper smoke.

I couldn't believe my luck. It was like something out of the movies! To me, my eldest brother was like the Godfather, and he had just given me the green light to join the mob. I enthusiastically thanked him, and he smiled again as I got out of the car and began to make my way back to the garage, intending to share my news with Phil. Before I could make it to the door, however, my eldest brother, now also out of the car, told me to wait. My mind raced, along with my heart. What now? Had he changed his mind? Was I not cut out for the group? He then sent one of his friends into the garage and told him to get me what he described as a half. His friend quickly returned and handed me an even larger bag with an even larger amount of skunk inside. I thanked him and then thanked my brother again. This was the moment I had been waiting for. Ever since I was a little boy, I had felt rejected and just wanted to be accepted – accepted by my eldest brother, accepted by my family, accepted by society.

I just wanted to be included and now my opportunity had finally arrived.

Before my brother left he took me to one side and quietly showed me how to divide the half-ounce of skunk into profitable amounts, explaining what to sell in order to make it worth my while. When I returned to the garage, I weighed the skunk; I had just under an ounce! The estimated street value of that amount was around £130. Phil sat and watched as I carefully weighed the half-ounce into four equal amounts. I saw he was captivated so, emboldened by my new-found responsibility, I seized the opportunity to capitalize on his interest.

'Want to buy some?' I asked.

'I don't have any money on me,' Phil replied reluctantly, before adding, 'but I can get it off my mum tomorrow and then pay you.'

I agreed without hesitation. I might have only recently started taking drugs, but I'd been around them for years, so I knew this was known in the business as ticking – giving someone drugs now in expectation of payment later. Looking back at Phil's smiling face, I knew he was a happy customer. What I didn't realize, however, was that giving Phil that eighth on tick was officially the start of my drug-dealing career. I had started that summer telling Phil I wanted to get a job. Now here I was with the first job I felt I could do.

I fully believe every person is responsible for their decisions, but looking back I was just a kid trying to belong, and after so many wrong turns, drug dealing was the only thing that felt right.

I WATCHED IT ALL UNFOLDING RIGHT BEFORE MY EYES LIKE A MOVIE.

CHAPTER SIX

Divided. If I could sum up my final years as a teenager in one word, this would be it. I spent my time in the garage dividing up drugs, all the while feeling divided myself. On the one hand, I had found something I was actually good at; I felt accepted, that I belonged. On the other hand, it was impossible to ignore the harsh reality: things in the garage were starting to spiral out of control and as much as I tried to press down my anxieties with drugs, things always found a way of coming to the surface.

My brother's already aggressive reputation was growing daily, and he was fast becoming known in more and more boroughs for his violent approach. His martial arts skills were not only taking on more strength – by now he was a fourth dan black belt in a branch of Kung Fu – but were being used in more contexts, most noticeably on the streets. If I had learnt anything from my first drug deal on tick to Phil, it was that not everyone pays back on time or at all – and my brother had begun pulling out all the stops to make sure they did. I began to wake up almost daily to hear about the fights he had participated in the night before; how he'd aggressively beaten people up on the streets – or worse, in the garage. There were times when I was out in town and strangers would come up to me and ask who I was; I looked so much like my brother that at times people would do a double-take when they passed me, thinking I was him. That wasn't so bad when their stares were filled with respect, but by now I had started to wonder whether these people were really his 'friends' at all. I grew increasingly anxious about going out of the house, always on guard when people approached me. If they weren't my brother's friends, maybe they were enemies?

Sadly, my brother's aggression wasn't used to protect me; it was used against me. One day, he and I got into an argument and he squared up to me, threatening me directly to my face. With no better ideas, I swore at him, but this was a mistake. Without a moment's hesitation, he began to chase me out of the garage, into the house and across the living room, where my father was sitting watching the news; now I was between a rock and a hard place. With bated breath, I watched as my father rose to protect me, or perhaps just to intimidate my brother, who soon backed down like a hyena that had spotted a lion.

My father shouted at the top of his voice, 'I'm going to close that garage *now*.' I'd never seen my brother run faster as he shot towards the garage to grab his stuff, and stash everything he needed in a backpack before my father could find out the full extent of what was going on in there. By the time my father had started nailing the garage door shut, my brothers and his friends were already walking up the dirt alley to freedom. I, however, felt more trapped than ever before – both physically and emotionally.

The self-condemnation that had long haunted me was never very far away, but the night of that argument it came back in full force. I knew my brother wasn't innocent, that my father's temper didn't help, but somehow I still felt responsible for the argument that had taken place. I felt that my brother had just started to accept me and now I had ruined everything. The already hostile atmosphere that filled the house notched up another level as I sat, still high from the skunk I had been smoking earlier, in an armchair across from my father. I watched anxiously as he sat huffing and puffing on the settee, occasionally bursting into aggressive fits of rage, shouting about how my brothers and I were no good. 'This whole damn family makes me sick,' he said as my mother got more and more upset.

As night fell, I retreated to the solitude of my room, too tired to gather my thoughts. This would be OK. We'd argued before. Everything would go back to normal. But was normal really any better? The thoughts rushed round and round my busy mind, and no matter how hard I tried I just couldn't relax, the events of the day playing over and over in my head. The hours soon passed, but there I was, lying in bed staring at the ceiling as the worry turned to guilt and then morphed back to concern. I knew in my gut that something bad was about to happen and I needed to be ahead of the game. Through this cocktail of emotion, only one coherent thought started to rise: I was pretty sure I had left a fairly large bag of cannabis in the pocket of my jeans, which were now slumped in a heap on the floor. I was almost certain this paranoia was just a natural symptom of all the drugs I'd taken, but it was really starting to take hold. Reluctantly, I decided to drag myself out of bed, walk across the cold and silent room and look for the cannabis. I scrabbled into the front pocket of my jeans and pulled out the bag of cannabis, but instead of feeling relief, a rush of panic filled my veins. Was I having a panic attack? Either way I knew I needed to hide the drugs – and *now*.

There I stood, in the middle of my small bedroom in the early hours of the morning with nothing but my underwear on, debating where to hide this rather large bag of skunk, with no idea as to *why* I felt this uncontrollable need to hide it. With blood coursing through my veins and my heart pounding in my chest, my eyes caught on a large framed poster of an old BMW 5 Series hung on the wall. With concern still clouding out everything else, I began to unscrew the bolts that held the frame on to the wall, rested the poster on the floor and flattened the bundle of cannabis as best as I could before sticking it to the back of the frame. Screwing the poster – and the drugs along with it – back on to the wall, I stood back to study it, adrenalin still pounding in my chest. Climbing back into bed, I closed my eyes and listened to my heartbeat finally beginning to slow: *beat, beat, beat, bang, bang, bang . . .* My eyes shot open as my body shot up. Somebody was at the door. At 4 a.m. in the morning. *Who the hell would be here at this time? No one good . . .*

I jumped out of bed and put on some clothes, rushing out of my room and downstairs as fast as I could. For a moment, my anxiety slowed – it was probably just my brother returning home from a night out. But as I neared the front door, I could hear an unfamiliar voice forcing its way into our home. It was the police. And they were there to search the place. Instinctively, I turned to head back upstairs and towards my bedroom, searching the room for any evidence of drugs laying around. With panic surging through my veins, I reached to grab a few roll-up papers from the floor before I heard the sound of heavy footsteps approaching. I knew the officer was only seconds away, so I stuffed the papers into a pair of my trainers discarded near the bed and stood up straight, just in time to see him standing in the doorway of my room, red-faced and breathing heavily.

He looked surprised to see me, but a little smile threatened to turn up the corners of his mouth as he realized that I was cornered in my room with no way to escape. My heart raced a thousand miles per hour, but not nearly as much as my mind. This was the first time our house had been searched by the police; I had never had such a direct encounter with them before, but this officer looked at like me as if I was a dime a dozen – just another good-for-nothing young man in need of sorting out. His tall, overweight stature shadowed over me as I shrank back on to my bed. I looked up at him – around mid-thirties, with fair thinning hair that sat in an awkward side parting. I didn't know him, but I remember thinking we were from two completely different worlds. *I bet he only applied to be a policeman so he could catch people like me,* I thought to myself. My family's general view of the police wasn't a very positive one, so if they had arrived in the middle of the night to visit us I knew it could be bad news, but the question was: how bad?

Pretending that I had just run upstairs to get my trainers, I reached down to pick up the right one and began to put it on. As I slipped it on, I felt the cigarette papers that I had stuffed into my trainer crush beneath my foot, and then the same happened as I slipped my left foot into the other.

The officer escorted me back downstairs and into the living room, where the detectives were explaining to my parents that my brother had been arrested. It felt like an out-of-body experience, staring at my father as he sat on his chair at the head of the dining room table while the police searched around him. My mother supervised while the accompanying female officer emptied the kitchen drawers of their belongings. She looked desperate, but then again, the situation was. She watched on helplessly as the police officers continued to empty every cupboard and every drawer, searching through the refrigerator and anything else that could be opened, even forcing open some things that at first refused to budge. My heart hurt as I watched my mother clearing up behind the officers, reassembling matchboxes of memories she had collected over the years as red-hot embarrassment coursed through me.

'All right, back to your room.' The officer who had escorted me downstairs was now forcing me back up them so that he could begin his search of my room – just when I thought it was over. With a single finger he signalled for me to lead the way and when we arrived in my bedroom he immediately began to search me, asking me to lift my arms while he patted me down. Finding nothing on me, he proceeded to pick up my clothes and empty my pockets before moving on to the TV stand opposite my bed and then searching under it. Every so often he would look at me in frustration and I would smile in return, the whole time praying that he wouldn't think to remove the massive poster I had stashed the cannabis behind.

Eventually, one of the detectives from downstairs came up to my bedroom to check how things were going. Disheartened, the officer who had been searching around sighed and walked the few short paces towards the doorway. I stood there watching, heart racing, while the two men stood shoulder to shoulder looking for a clue – anything that would point them towards the concealment that they knew they had frustratingly missed.

'We're not getting anywhere here,' one detective said, his frustration palpable. Sure they'd missed something, they began to make their way downstairs. As soon as they were out of sight, my legs crumbled beneath me. I sat, heart throbbing, roll-up papers in my shoes, as I tried to catch my breath. Sitting on the edge of my bed, I tried to listen as the detectives talked to my parents for a moment longer, then I heard the door shutting behind them. Silence fell upon the house as we listened to the doors of the unmarked police car outside slam shut, the engine start and the vehicle slowly disappear into the night.

I waited for a few moments before nervously creeping into my parents' bedroom and looking out of the window to make sure that the police had gone. From downstairs, I could hear my parents talking to one another, supporting each other. Somehow the tension from the arguments that had taken place that day had evaporated in the heat of something else, something much bigger. The police randomly searching our house had somehow given my parents common ground to speak again. The guilt I had been feeling before the police arrived drifted away; I was so scared that my father was going to explode and hit my mother.

Somehow the surprise of what had taken place that night bonded us all again. Looking back now, I can see just how bad things must have been for a police search to make them better, but novelty has a way of doing that.

Sadly, what felt surprising then was soon to become commonplace, as the police proceeded to search our house time and time again from that night on. Truthfully speaking, I lost count of how many times they randomly showed up in the early hours of the morning, demanding to enter the premises and search our home. Maybe that doesn't sound like a 'home' to you at all, but for me it was the only home I'd ever known. Although something significant was about to shift.

Later that same night, I woke up to hear the sound of my parents discussing what could have happened to my brother. He still hadn't been back to the house since he'd left the garage before my father could get him, and I was pretty sure that his homecoming wasn't going to be like that of the prodigal son. Hour after hour passed and with each passing minute, I knew my father's reaction to his return was going to be even worse.

When he eventually arrived at our house, looking distressed and worse for wear, I held my breath. Surely, my father was about to hit the roof, attack him, teach him a lesson. Instead, my father said nothing. He just sat there on the sofa, with one leg up and his hands clenched firmly behind his head, his thick brown-rimmed glasses falling down his nose as he watched the news. He didn't even *look* at my brother. He didn't look at anyone. I watched with bated breath; I was so sure the eruption was about to come. But it never did. My mind raced. Why wasn't he saying anything?

Had my dad changed for the better? Or was he simply losing the will to fight? Or worse, the will to live?

As my brother walked past my father, I followed him all the way up the stairs, trying to say hello, desperately seeking some sort of reassurance.

'It's your fault this all happened,' he snapped, shooting me daggers. I didn't even know the full story of what had happened, but I knew he was right. This *was* all my fault. It was my fault my parents were fighting. It was my fault my brother got into trouble. It was my fault the police had searched our house. It was my fault my father had given up.

Forcing my legs towards my bedroom, I felt useless, the thick fog of depression reminding me of just how worthless I was. Looking around my small box room, I began a search of my own. I needed something to comfort my anxiety, but I knew I'd only find it in the garage.

By the time my eldest brother came to visit, things had died down and we were once again in the garage. Almost as soon as I'd found out that my brother had been charged with some sort of possession of drugs and bailed, we were 'celebrating' this news in the garage. I was too young to understand the seriousness of the case and listening to my brother and his friends excitedly relaying story after story of how he had been caught, I wasn't entirely sure it was a bad thing. As I sat and listened to my brothers laughing, smoking and discussing what he should have done to avoid being caught, I couldn't help but feel it was glamorous and fun. I was just happy to be invited into the antics, but sadly even that was about to come to an end.

Shortly after my brother's arrest, he moved out to a small studio flat, and my social life in the garage came to an abrupt halt. Now it was just me, my parents and my cannabis habit, which was growing and growing. I would visit my brother's flat almost daily to pick up my drugs, but no matter how strong the hit, it wasn't able to fill the very real needs I had inside.

Things were changing rapidly, none more so than my father's health. Though my father's lack of reaction to my brother's arrest had seemed odd to me at the time, it was now starting to make sense: he was getting older and weaker by the day. Maybe after years of fighting and fighting, the strength inside him was finally running dry.

Shortly after my brother moved out, my mother and I began going to work with my father to help out. We couldn't do much, but for some reason he seemed to appreciate what we could do, and unexpectedly began paying me £40 a week. He must have known what I was spending this hard-earned money on, because one day, when we were sitting in the van, he looked across at me from the driver's seat and in his weathered Jamaican accent calmly said, 'Listen, Claud, don't smoke the cannabis.' Feeling rumbled, I prepared myself to go on the defensive, denying that I'd ever tried it or saying that I had but I'd finally stopped, but the onslaught never came. Instead, my father continued to give me his calm but strangely caring advice. He explained that smoking cannabis wasn't any good for me, before going on to share why he had never been a cannabis smoker himself. It was one of the few rare intimate moments that my father and I ever shared. Just him and me, sitting in the van chatting.

I didn't know it at the time, but going to work with my father and mother was a blessing in disguise. The few months that we all worked together allowed us to feel like a family, albeit one that had already been through so much violence, pain and disappointment. There was always something to laugh about and it was good to see my parents enjoying each other's company. My father would often sit to the side and watch while I did bits of work here and there, screwing kitchen units together or putting up plasterboard. At lunchtimes, if we hadn't brought anything with us to eat, he would give me some money and send me to get some fish and chips. Standing there in the shop with my dusty and paint-stained clothes on, I felt a strange sense of fulfilment and self-worth. I would walk proudly back to the job with the bag of warm fish and chips under my arm, looking forward to the praise that awaited my arrival.

As my father's health deteriorated further, my brother-in-law began working with us too. He was also of Jamaican descent and, understanding my father's character, they got on very well indeed.

One day they both arrived home from work early and I was surprised to hear them talking in hushed tones downstairs.

'What's going on?' I asked as soon as I'd made my way into the room.

'Pops fell over,' my brother-in-law replied sheepishly.

'What do you mean, fell over?' I asked, panic prickling up the hairs on my arms. I looked to my mother; the concern was written across every inch of her face.

'We were at the builders' merchant,' my father explained as he smiled, showing no signs of weakness, even though his body was. 'I lost my footing and took a fall. My leg a' hurt me,' he continued in his familiar thick Jamaican accent while rubbing his leg.

I looked across at my mother, who remained silent throughout. This was the man who had attacked her countless times now visibly getting weaker before her and yet she still found it hard to see.

'You all think I'm getting old,' my father joked, and we all tried to laugh it off even though it was true. Following his fall, my father never drove his van again and he soon began complaining of headaches. Things slowed down dramatically at work, and for most of the day my father would find something to sit on and just give direction. It was strange to see; my father had been the hardest worker I had ever known. He'd been able to drive a six-inch nail home with two or three blows of a hammer and now here he was, too tired to sit upright. The deterioration of my father's health came unexpectedly quickly, so much so that at first I thought it was simply a result of his fall. The headaches came quicker and stronger until he simply had no strength left at all and he could no longer get out of bed, let alone go to work.

Day after day and night after night, my mother nursed my father relentlessly, only leaving his side to fix lunch or dinner. I watched it all unfolding right before my eyes like a movie. The house that had once been filled with so much colour and chaos was often silent, so silent that if you listened carefully you could swear the silence created a sound of its own. After a few more days, my mother gathered all of the family together at the house. It was nice to see everyone in one place for the first time in years, my brothers, my sister, my brother-in-law gathering into the small space. The sadness of the situation made our reunion bittersweet; we all knew why we were there.

I was still 16 when my father passed away and to this day his death has a great effect on me. My father was the strong one, the forceful one, the presence we all respected and at times despised. But he was also the glue that held our family together. He was the padlock on our chain. Though his discipline was dangerous, it was also the thing that forced us closer; if my family members hadn't seen one another in a while, it was my father who would demand that everyone meet up for a BBQ. Of course, when my father was demanding it, everyone knew to turn up. Though my mother is the strongest and most loyal woman I know, it was my father's bravery and strength that sustained us, and ever since his death our family has fallen apart. There were times when I hated him, when I knew his behaviour created so much tension that it stopped our various houses from becoming homes. And yet his fearlessness right up until his last breath, coupled with the rare tender moments we shared together towards the end of his days, will always stay with me. In spite of everything, I still loved my father; I always will.

I DIDN'T KNOW THEN
THAT THIS YEARNING
WAS FOR SOMETHING
THIS WORLD COULD
NEVER SATISFY.

CHAPTER SEVEN

I had always wanted something else, something *more*, but my father's death sent this wanting into overdrive. After so many years of feeling like I'd been dealt a bad set of cards, I wanted to somehow pay life back for all the hurt it had handed out to me, but against everything inside me that told me not to trust others, I still desperately wanted to belong.

Shortly after turning 16 I had begun to regularly travel back and forth from our home in Surbiton to Tooting, in the hope of finding some of my old school friends, and this didn't stop after my father passed away. On reflection, I can see now that I was searching for some sort of identity. I had found it there in the garage alongside my brothers. I had found it sitting in the van with my father, finally feeling I had a caring father for once. And yet it all too quickly drifted away. This time I was going to find my identity properly – not in sleepy Surbiton, but on the streets of Tooting, in the place I had grown up. But there was one key difference. Where drugs had been a present but peculiar idea to my childhood mind, now they were tangibly real and all too accessible.

The cannabis availability in Tooting was unbelievable and very soon it wasn't just old familiar friends I was reconnecting with – I was making new ones. My contact list of users and suppliers grew rapidly; it felt like everyone knew somebody who sold drugs. Though my brothers introduced me to drugs in the garage, I was now getting to know them up close and personal, and I quickly began to learn about the business – the people I could trust and those I definitely, categorically couldn't. Before long, I added a new habit to my list: catching the 71 bus from Surbiton to Kingston and the 57 bus from Kingston to Tooting every single day in my latest bid to belong.

I enjoyed the multicultural community that Tooting offered; there were so many interesting characters and instead of sticking out like a sore thumb, I learnt how to mix into the community hustle and bustle. I knew it was important to understand how to move and carry yourself in the neighbourhoods; if my brothers had taught me anything, it was that reputation was everything. The only people you didn't want to have a bad reputation with were the police. After seeing what had happened to my brothers, my biggest worry at the time was avoiding being stopped and searched by police officers on the beat – something that would happen about three or four times on any given day. It happened so frequently that eventually the officers started writing receipts to tell the other officers that I had already been searched. Their behaviour towards me only further confirmed what I already thought: they didn't like me; they weren't like me. In fact, they were against me.

The police aside, the summers I spent in Tooting were great. We'd hang out in a local park and smoke skunk while sharing stories of what had happened to whom recently. It was all about names, networks and notoriety, and I soon met a lot of local 'street stars'. These 'stars' were usually older, drove nice cars and wore expensive jewellery. These guys were always extremely fashionable and yet had a style of their own, often wearing very expensive jeans, the newest of trainers, or the newest tracksuits with a gold chain or bracelet worn on display for everyone to see. They would often speed up the streets of Tooting, sounding the car horn as they drove by. Everyone in our group wanted to be like them, and I was no exception. And, unlike the youth club leader or the footballers I had idolized in the past, these street stars felt more in reach. I gravitated towards them and in turn they often gravitated to me.

One of the street stars I became close to was a chap we called Yella. He was a real character; he was super funny, drove a super-fast moped and sold some pretty super skunk! I used to buy up to £30 worth of skunk from Yella every day, and even though I was the one buying from him, he taught me so much about selling. Yella was a great businessman, even at the young age of 17; he would buy extra-fluffy skunk so that the portions looked bigger, and although you always knew that you were getting less than you'd paid for, it was easier to accept when you saw what appeared to be a larger portion in your bag. This, and other savvy ideas, made Yella a great drug dealer, and he had more pairs of trainers than anyone else I knew. In later life, I would of course learn much of what the Bible says about wealth and possessions, namely: 'You cannot serve both God and money' (Matthew 6.24), but at the time, we felt that an identity could be bought.

I remember the first time I went to Yella's house; his room was so crammed full of designer trainer boxes that you could barely open the door to force your way in. Even though my mother had always tried to make sure I didn't go without, I'd never seen wealth like it. Yella wore a different pair of trainers every day, always matching whatever tracksuit he had on. Or he wore expensive denim jeans from Japan, with one pair costing hundreds of pounds.

As I spent more time with Yella I began to notice that he always carried at least one credit card. Up until that point, I had thought the only people who used credit cards were rich white people – definitely not 17-year-old drug dealers from the slums. To say I was intrigued was a massive understatement and I eventually built up the courage to ask Yella about how he managed to get someone to give him so many credit cards. He then told me about credit card fraud.

Looking back, I feel like his response should have surprised me, but at the time all I felt was excitement. My frustrations with the police, with my family, with *life*, had only grown, and the tiny seed of revenge that had at some point planted itself within me was by now blossoming into fruition. Though I know my forgiveness has been hard-won and for many this kind of fraud crosses every moral line, at the time I just remember thinking that Yella had everything I thought I wanted, and credit card fraud was the way to get it.

Yella explained the process and had all the contacts we needed to reprogram the cards; it seemed simple enough. The hardest part was finding the cards themselves. I was the only one in my immediate circle who even had a bank account let alone a credit card. Once I knew what to look for, I soon got my hands on some credit card documentation, but without cards to reprogram, it was pointless!

'Couldn't you just reprogram my debit card?' I asked Yella one day.

'I can, but you'll get caught as soon as you go to use it,' he cautioned.

I wouldn't listen. I sat there patiently watching while Yella reprogramed two other credit cards for his own use, and finally he reached over and took the documentation and my own personal card out of my hands and within a few short minutes it was all done. 'If you're ever trying to use the card and the cashier calls for authorization, just walk away,' Yella explained to me seriously. 'Walk away *quickly*.'

'Right,' I said, feeling nervous but not nearly nervous enough to turn back.

'And if the cashier calls for security,' Yella went on, '*RUN!*'

The first time I used the card I was so nervous I could barely even speak, but after a while it became like second nature to me. Everywhere I went I used the card, mainly just for confidence purposes. Eventually, the card got declined for the first time. I was just about to make a run for it, but then the cashier happily handed the card back to me. I went to get more documentation and then straight back to Yella to get the card reprogramed again. My habit of fraudulent credit card use became more excessive and with it my confidence grew. Sadly, my greed grew with it.

I soon began to take more risks with the value of items, and I felt my reputation grow with each and every purchase. We were young and thirsty: thirsty for riches, thirsty for success, thirsty for everything that life had cheated us of. I wanted what I felt was owed to me and I wanted it immediately. I had tried to do things the right way, but felt that bullying, racism, disappointment and setbacks had held me back. I just wanted to move forward.

In the years after giving my life to Jesus and being embraced into a loving church family, I would learn the role of encouragement and affirmation in building up confidence in who we are and what we are called to do. At this point in time, however, what was being encouraged in me was my life of crime. My successful stint of cheating the system through credit card fraud had won me 'friends' and a reputation, and now I wanted more. I didn't know then that this yearning was for something this world could never satisfy. Like many young people today, I thought I could fill this God-shaped hole with money; I knew it was time to develop the 'family business'.

Following in my eldest brother's footsteps in supplying drugs seriously was harder than I thought. Ever since we'd not been meeting in the garage, my supply of marijuana had grown inconsistent, as had his contacts. I had to start from scratch, building up my own customer base. Like any supply chain, you rely on those above you to be able to deliver, which was risky business, but then I had grown up around high risk, high reward. I thought my luck was starting to change when I met a guy who was willing to 'tick' me ounces, charging more than the going rate, but allowing me the time to sell it and get the money before paying him back. Everything went swimmingly for a number of months, but as soon as his product ran out, so did mine. The time soon came for me to pay up. The man began applying pressure, looking to collect a large outstanding payment. I knew I was £500 short. I fully intended to pay everything that was owed to him, but when I heard about the threats he was making to hurt me, I felt the damage was already done. If there was one thing I had learnt from my father, it was to not be intimidated, so I refused to repay him and called his bluff: now he'd have to follow through on the threats he was making or look weak. I don't share this story with you out of a place of pride, but simply to show how fearless I had become: I really didn't care if I got hurt. I was hurting enough already.

I still felt socially rejected from society and in the moments when I wasn't buying, selling or doing drugs, my demons of self-doubt and my insecurities of inadequacy would regularly return at any given time of day. Although I was still plagued by these demons, my new-found 'friends' on the streets were making me see that I wasn't the only one with them. We were all nothing more than a bunch of social misfits, but at least we 'fit' together. With these people, I found the sense of community I was searching for. At the core of so many of my issues, and those experienced by the young people I have worked with since knowing Jesus, was the desire to fit in, to belong, to be accepted. And in my circles at the time, that meant pushing the boundaries and always chasing more.

I remember hanging around with a couple of brothers from Brixton, who had a reputation locally that I and others admired. They were always pushing the boundaries: when we were driving mopeds, they drove faster ones. When we were driving faster mopeds, they bought cars. They were so cool and seemed to like hanging around with me too and, if you've picked up on anything from my story so far, you will know that being accepted mattered to me, often more than my morals.

One rainy night, I got a call from one of my closest friends asking if I could give him a lift. Keen to please, I said yes and agreed to drop him wherever he needed to go. It was a darker night than normal, and something didn't feel right, but I ignored my uncomfortable feeling and continued on to my friend's house. Shortly after arriving, I rang my friend's mobile and told him that I was outside, and he came down almost immediately. As he got into the car, I noticed that he was carrying a fairly large sports bag, but I didn't think anything of it. As I turned the key in the ignition, I received a phone call from my eldest brother, who frantically asked whether I had any drugs on me. I told him that I did, and he quickly advised that I didn't drive around with them. I agreed not to, but the lack of commitment in my voice must have been obvious, as he soon began to raise his.

'Go straight home,' he ordered down the phone before explaining that he'd had some kind of premonition that I was going to get caught. He didn't often speak like this and I was worried, really worried. I finished the conversation with my eldest brother and immediately pulled the car over.

'What's wrong?' my friend in the car asked. I told him everything and soon he was offering to hide the drugs I had on me somewhere in his house. After a few minutes, my friend was back, rainwater trickling down his arm and dripping off the sleeve of his black waterproof jacket. It was a very dark night and the rain was coming down so heavily, but reluctantly I pulled away.

As we headed towards Brixton Hill, a car sped up behind us with its full beam on. I looked in the rear-view mirror, but the lights of the car behind were so bright I couldn't make out who it was. The windscreen wipers were on full power, banging back and forth as they wrestled with the giant raindrops and I wrestled with my anxious thoughts. Soon those thoughts got the better of me. As I waited to pull out on to Brixton Hill and anxiety surged through my veins, I saw a gap in the traffic and took my opportunity. Slamming my foot on the accelerator pedal, the car screamed as its wheels spun in the rain and I left the bright headlamps in the distance. Moments later, they were closing in on us again. I took the next left; so did the car behind. Accelerating harder, the sound of police sirens filled me with dread. Fearfully, I looked in the rear-view mirror, confirming my worst fear: the bright headlamp beams were now accompanied by blue flashing lights and sirens. My heart banged like a bass drum; we had to pull over. By the time I took off my seat belt and unlocked the door to get out, the police officers were already at our doors. What I didn't know at the time was that my friend currently had a warrant out for his arrest and as soon as the officers saw him, they recognized him and called for back-up immediately. One of the officers took me by the arm, directing me to wait over by the fence.

'I remember you,' the ash-grey haired officer said. 'You're the one that used to always ride the moped, aren't you?'

Heart throbbing in my chest, I remained quiet.

'That's right, you were always up front leading the pack,' the officer went on.

I hadn't ever been arrested before; how could he possibly know who I was? The thought should have been a warning: he knew I was in the wrong crowd. Instead, I could feel my ego naively expanding. I was part of the gang. I belonged there. Not only that, I was leading the pack . . .

'That thing was bloody fast,' the police officer mused on, as I felt a sense of pride soften my body. 'How fast did it go? That *was* yours, right?'

I should have remained silent, but the recognition was too much to resist. 'That's right,' I beamed. 'That was my moped.'

The officer's face changed instantly. 'I've been waiting to catch you for a long time!' he said with vengeance in his voice.

Any ego I had been feeling in that moment was gone. He began reading me my rights and I knew I was in serious trouble. I watched on as one of the officers inquisitively removed my friend's large sports bag from the car.

'Do you have a driving licence?' the officer asked me.

I nodded, even though I didn't.

'Do you have insurance for the vehicle?'

I nodded again, even though I didn't.

'What kind of cover do you have?'

'Third Party, Fire and Theft,' I said, worry evident in my voice. As I stood there waiting, I noticed two young lads in the distance watching the kerfuffle taking place. They soon decided to ride over on their bikes, spectating from a couple of yards away.

'What's happening, mate?' one of them shouted out. 'Are you getting done?'

I tried my best to front it out, but all I could do was shrug my shoulders. Suddenly 'leading the pack' didn't feel like the best place to be any more. The police officers put my friend and me in the back of separate vehicles and as we sped off for the police station, the dark thoughts that were never too far from the surface started to rise. I thought about my mother, about all we'd been through together, and how I had let her down. I thought about my father, about my childhood and my family.

All of a sudden, the doors to the van opened and I was directed to get out. As I climbed out, I caught a glimpse of my friend being escorted into the station in the distance and somehow felt strangely comforted, such was my trust in the people I respected. The officers escorted me into the reception area and I randomly saw the mother of another friend of mine who worked at the front desk. Far from being concerned or ashamed by her being there, I saw it as a bonus; I knew that she would go straight home and tell her son that I had been arrested and by the next morning he would have told everyone, magnifying my profile within our social group. This line of thought may sound crazy to you, but back then, before I found my faith – or, rather, faith found me – this kind of stuff mattered.

Once in the depths of the police station, things went from bad to worse. As the officers closed the iron door and locked me in the urine-infested cell, I tried to prepare myself for what was to come, but overwhelmed by emotion, I couldn't even settle. A wave of self-doubt and insecurity washed over me, making it impossible to sit still; I began anxiously pacing back and forth. The cell was cold and empty but for a seat-less toilet and a thin blue mattress resting on a block, apparently my bed. As I paced, the scent of urine filled my nostrils and I began to sweat, my dark thoughts becoming increasingly impossible to control. I began to panic and reached for the button to the left of the cell door, which I assumed would call for assistance. Nothing happened. I waited a little longer and then pressed it again. Still nothing happened. Then I pressed the button again and again and again. The silence was unbearable. Growing more and more frustrated, I leapt forward to kick the cell door. I kicked it again and again. Suddenly the flap on the cell door swung open and the unfamiliar and angry eyes of an officer stared back at me.

'What do you want?' the officer snarled aggressively. 'This isn't a hotel; we don't come when you call!'

'I need a cigarette,' I said as calmly as I could.

'See this as an opportunity to stop smoking,' the officer jeered sarcastically.

'When am I going home?' I shouted desperately. I knew it was still Friday night, but I had no idea how long I had been in the cell.

'Oh,' the officer smirked, 'you won't be going home. You'll be staying here until Monday, then you'll be going straight to court where you'll be remanded.' Before I could reply, he slammed the iron flap shut.

My heart hammered, my throat closed, the room span. *I'm not going home? I'm not going home?!* What the officer had just said played over and over in my mind. In the silence of the cell, I broke down. I had no energy left. I couldn't fight any longer. I had struggled to deal with things in my past, but for the first time in my life not a soul was there to help me. Not my mother, not my brothers, not the youth leader, not my friends.

I dropped to my knees as tears filled my eyes. Resting my elbows on the bed, I put my hands together and decided to pray. With my eyes closed, I begged and pleaded desperately for God to get me out of this situation. I poured my heart out and in great distress repeated my request time and time again. I had prayed occasionally for things in the past, like for my father not to hit my mother, but this felt different. I prayed with a sincerity that I hadn't felt before.

Eventually, I got up from my knees, and lying on the bed in exhaustion soon fell into a really deep and peaceful sleep. I would later learn the verse in the Bible where the apostle Paul, who also prayed while in gaol, encourages believers to 'not be anxious about anything, but in every situation, by prayer and petition, with thanksgiving, present your requests to God. And the peace of God, which transcends all understanding, will guard your hearts and your minds in Christ Jesus' (Philippians 4.6–7). Unlike Paul, I was not in prison for sharing the gospel – I was in prison because of my own choices – but the fact that God still heard my prayers and still granted me peace that night shows just how merciful he is.

A few hours later, the cell door opened and two officers walked in, waking me from my sleep. The leading officer briefly introduced himself before abruptly asking, 'So why do you think you deserve to go home?'

'Because I didn't do anything,' I barked in response. They left as quickly as they had arrived, and I was alone again. More time passed before another person spoke to me – this time someone offering me some breakfast through the flap in the door. His kindness was refreshing, but I refused rigidly, tears threatening to fill my eyes.

I spent the next few hours in reflection and prayer. What did Monday have in store for me? What was going to happen at court? Would they be sentencing immediately? How long would I be sentenced to? Which prison would they send me to? These and many other questions raced through my mind. I found myself praying against each worry, that God would help me, that I'd be able to go home. As I was deep in thought, the cell door unexpectedly opened, and an officer entered the cell before telling me it was time for my interview. I was led out of the cell and down the passage into the main reception area, where two detectives were waiting for me. Beckoning me into the interview room, one of the detectives directed me to take a seat on a chair positioned next to a brown desk, while the two of them sat on the other side. One of them pressed the red button on a tape recorder and swiftly began to quiz me: where was I going and what was I doing? Did I know who the guy was in the car with me? What were our intentions? Did we have anything on us?

'We were on our way to a mate's house,' I explained, but the detectives wouldn't accept my answer and quickly grew frustrated.

All of a sudden, one of them produced the large sports bag that my friend had been carrying when he got into my car, and slammed it on to the desk. 'Have you seen this before?' he asked.

I shook my head.

'It was in your car,' he said, before emptying the contents on to the desk. I sat motionless as pack after pack of marijuana was lined out along the desk. For a moment, it felt as if everything was happening in slow motion, as if all the sound and air had been sucked out of the room, until

I heard the detective's words breaking through: 'Who does all of this belong to?'

'I don't know,' I replied desperately.

The detective wouldn't accept it. It was in my car and therefore, he reasoned, the cannabis must belong to me. On and on the questions came until all of a sudden the interview seemed to end as quickly as it had started.

'Your friend says it's his and that you knew nothing about it,' one of the detectives explained, though he seemed far from convinced. Still, I was going to be released.

I followed them back into the main reception area, where I saw my friend waiting alongside another officer. Before I walked out of the station, leaving him behind, he stood up to shake my hand. 'See you soon,' I said.

I didn't know then that he was going to prison for years.

I WOULD NEED GOD
TO MEET ME AGAIN
AND AGAIN BEFORE I
FINALLY GAVE MY LIFE
TO HIM.

CHAPTER EIGHT

It was a difficult time for me when my friend went to prison. Frankly speaking, I missed him. He was one of my best friends; I'd hung out with him every day. His going to prison was to be a turning point for me. After my hours spent in that cell, praying on my hands and knees for God to intervene, I should have walked from that station a changed man. I should have taken the prison sentence of one of my best friends as a warning, just like my eldest brother's time in prison when I was young. And yet I didn't. I was weak. I was in too deep. I would need God to meet me again and again before I finally gave my life to him.

My friend who had gone to prison was only a teenager, but he had taught me a lot – a lot about myself, but also a lot about survival. We always used to say that we didn't care, that no matter what happened we would simply shrug it off. And, somewhere along the line, I had come to believe that. Looking back now, I see this apathy was a way to cushion the pain. If I acted like I wasn't hurt, I could fool myself – along with everyone else – that it didn't. As a result, it didn't take me long to shake off the shock of getting arrested. After all, I was getting deeper into the business of drug dealing and by now had become far too accustomed to the lifestyle to let it go easily. I embraced the lack of responsibility that I had; I enjoyed it. The feelings of rejection that I carried around, and my insecurity, were lodged in my heart, but the risks of drug dealing gave me enough of a buzz and sense of identity to mask the truth.

By the time I was 19 years old I had a convertible sports car, which I would purposefully show off at the traffic lights, bringing the electric top down as onlookers marvelled at what was then relatively new technology. At the time, money was not something to be shared or given away, not something I saw as God's provision to be generous with. No, back then I saw money as power. I was such a cocky young punk that I thought I was in control, when really my insecurities meant I was constantly catering to people's expectations and behaviours towards me. If I walked into a bar with a beautiful girl, and a bunch of guys turned around to brazenly check her out, I'd buy a bottle or two of champagne and make sure that I popped them right in front of the guys. I meet many young people now who are just like I was back then and I understand that beneath the bravado there are usually countless reasons why those individuals feel they need to have wealth or be envied in order to feel worthy.

From that point on, life was a rollercoaster filled with ups and downs. I remember one night I had just finished visiting a girl who lived in a flat on an estate in Croydon. As I was exiting her block, I walked out of the main door towards my car and saw a police car drive past very slowly, an officer inside the car making eye contact with me as he went. I soon lost sight of it, but suspected that they had pulled up just behind the exit to the car park. Knowing I was carrying drugs on me, I instantly called up to the girl I had just left and asked her to look out of her window and tell me if the police were still waiting. The girl reassured me that everything was fine and suggested that I was just being paranoid, but I had a feeling something was going to happen, so before getting into my car I decided to roll the paraphernalia up into the waist of my boxer shorts, tucking it firmly down into the crotch of my jeans. I then got into my car, locked the doors, lit a spliff and started the engine.

As I drove out of the estate, the police car that I had seen a few moments earlier pulled out from behind a bush and began to follow me. With fear clouding my vision, I slowed to about 20 miles per hour, put the spliff in the ashtray, and started repeatedly praying out loud: 'Please God, make everything be OK. Please don't let me get arrested. Again.'

Eventually, the police officers put on the three blue lights and pulled me over. As I got out of the car, I was so scared that I began to shake uncontrollably. After taking my details one of the officers asked me to step on the kerb and explained that he was going to search me. As he started to pat me down, he questioned why I was shaking so badly. 'You haven't got anything to hide, have you?'

This whole damn lifestyle was about hiding. Hiding from my hurts. Hiding from responsibility. Hiding from hope that could so easily disappoint. 'I'm not shaking,' I lied; by now I was used to lying to police officers. 'I'm cold.'

The officer ran his hands along my arms, up towards my armpits, before doing the same to my legs. My heart hammered as I realized how close he was to finding the hidden paraphernalia stashed in my groin area, but he never did. After he had searched me, the other one searched my car. All of a sudden I remembered the spliff in the ashtray; that would be more than enough to warrant them taking me to the police station for a strip search. I waited silently, expecting the officer to emerge from the car with the spliff in hand, but to my surprise he got out empty-handed. They reluctantly told me it was all right for me to go.

'*Thank you*,' I said joyfully as I turned to walk away.

'Why are you thanking us?' one of them asked with suspicion. 'Makes me think that we're letting you go and we shouldn't be.'

'No, not at all, officer,' I replied without a moment's hesitation. 'I'm just thanking you because some officers stop me and make life difficult for me.'

'Well, we're just a couple of guys with a job to do,' he said.

'Exactly, officer!' I beamed. 'You guys are proper police officers doing a proper job!'

'Off you go,' he said, signalling suspiciously towards my car.

I didn't waste any more time. Rushing to the car, I drove away and reaching to open my ashtray, I was surprised to find the giant spliff still lying there in the exact position that I had left it. I drove on for a moment, wondering if God had heard me and answered my prayers, just like after I was arrested and let go. Surely God wouldn't answer the prayers of someone who deserved to get into trouble? But for some reason, ever since my arrest, I had been praying more and more and was convinced someone was listening. My belief in God, whoever or whatever he was, had definitely begun to grow. Unfortunately, my ego and arrogance were growing too. Without another thought, I reached for the spliff and lit it.

By the time I was 19, I had begun seeing a girl a couple of years older than me. Outwardly, I looked like I had grown up, but inwardly I was still the same insecure young kid just trying to find my feet and discover my identity. After all the lies I had been told and been telling up until this point, it may not surprise you to hear that I couldn't trust her. But it turned out I was right not to trust her, as I soon found out that she had been talking to a lot of older local guys behind my back. These guys already had plenty of reasons to want to cause me harm, and they had a serious reputation that made me sure they wouldn't hesitate to follow through with their threats. I decided to stick it out, but could feel things spiralling out of control.

Around this time, I remember sitting in my car when I noticed an older drug dealer approaching in my left wing mirror. Before I could stop him, he was opening my passenger door and tumbling in. I had never spoken to him before but knew perfectly well who he was. I don't know what surprised me more: the fact that he had got into my car or that he actually knew of me. A couple of years earlier, my ego would have soared at the fact that he did; reputation and notoriety were everything. But by now, even the highs of drug dealing were beginning to be laced with fear and doubt.

'Here, take this, fam,' he said before I could ask him what he was doing. Reaching into his jacket pocket, he produced a cannabis sample.

'And take man's number as well. I'm about, in it.'

I cooperated, taking the number and reassuring him that I would. In reality, I had no intention of doing so. Truthfully speaking, I may have looked the part sat there in my designer leather jacket, but I was barely keeping my head above water. I was struggling financially. I had debts that I just couldn't pay and any money I did receive I spent before I got it. And to make matters even worse, drama had started to follow me. Where I had once found my community in the parks and streets of Tooting, I now felt I had more enemies than friends. Some older guys I didn't even know, from a different area, had seen me out and about and decided that they wanted to make my life difficult. Word was getting around and other people were adding fuel to the fire. I was on my own and didn't know how to handle the situation at the time but knew that it would erupt sooner or later.

The good days of drinking and laughing in the park seemed a long way away. Now, almost daily, bad things would happen. Where I had grown up treading on eggshells so as to not anger my dad, I now found myself constantly on edge through my own doing. One evening I had parked my car on this girl's estate and popped into her flat. I didn't intend to stay long, but while I was in her flat I couldn't stop looking out of her window to check on my car. I had parked it on her estate a million times before and nothing had happened, but this evening I just had a funny feeling that something bad was going to happen. I got up and looked out of her window yet again. Everything was fine.

'What's wrong?' she asked. I explained the uneasy feeling that I just couldn't shake. I got up to check the car again.

This time, as I approached the window and looked out, I saw a guy sitting in the front seat of my car looking through the glove box. Instinctively, I called out of the window before making my way down the stairs to the car park. By the time I arrived downstairs my heart was racing; who was in my car?

I burst through the ground-floor iron door, and it slammed back against the redbrick wall. I hadn't realized how hard I'd pushed it. Adrenalin rushed through my body as I made my way around the block of flats towards the car park. As I arrived at the entrance of the estate, I saw the guy I had spotted in my car. He was a tall, fairly well-built ginger-haired guy, now about to get into another car that had seemingly brought him here. Apprehensively, I made my way across the road from the estate and towards the ginger guy. I was a couple of feet away when to my surprise he swiftly turned around and met me with a hammer in his hand, poised and ready to swing. I looked into his eyes.

Only a couple of seconds passed before I leapt forward, grabbing a handful of his clothing. As we tussled with one another aggressively, our bodies slammed against the small dirty car he had been about to get into. Struggling to gain control over one another we broke loose and even though I was out-armed, I wanted to make him pay for breaking into my car. In desperation I leapt forward again, this time in the hope of grabbing the hammer still in his hands. We wrestled for a few more seconds before breaking loose again. Taking a few steps back, I distanced myself from the hammer in his hands. Then the ginger guy turned, opened the door to the car and jumped in, directing the driver to leave. The driver revved the engine as I ran out of the way. The tyres screeched as the car pulled away.

With a million thoughts rushing through my mind I made my way back across the road towards my car in the estate car park. Just as I was crossing, a police van pulled up and I sensed eyes looking at me. Soon, some officers got out and asked me what was going on. I tried to explain how someone had just broken into my car, but they seemed more interested in the scuffle that had taken place. I knew I was in the wrong for so many things, but it felt like I just couldn't catch a break.

From then on, things seemed to go from bad to worse. Just a few weeks after this incident, I was driving my girlfriend back to her flat. We arrived at a crossroads on the way, and I was slowly pulling out when I saw an old Toyota MR2 speeding towards the passenger side of the car. Time slowed down as my life flashed before my eyes. I had thought that was just an expression people said, until the moments immediately before the car collided with us at breakneck speed. I can still remember the girl's screams as the Toyota powerfully ploughed into the passenger side of the car, turning it over on impact and trapping my right hand under the side of the car. Through the broken window, I watched as the driver of the Toyota got out and ran away. Pain seared through me as I lay there trying to figure out how I was going to release my arm from under the car just as the smell of petrol roused me from my haze. We needed to get out. And *fast*. My girlfriend, in the passenger seat, must have followed my eyes as they looked around to see where the smell was coming from and landed on the stream of petrol leaking along the side of the car. She screamed and screamed as I tried to remain calm; I knew that I had to free my trapped arm and get out of the car immediately. As the car rocked back and forth, I tried my best to pull my arm out from under the door, but the more I pulled the more I cut my arm on the scattered glass from the window.

Eventually, after several attempts, I managed to free my arm, but my hands and fingers were extremely bloody and swollen. Instinctively, I reached up, grabbing at the keys that were still in the ignition of the car, and thankfully managed to turn the engine off. Meanwhile, my girlfriend was still strapped into the passenger seat and screaming hysterically. I reached over and unlocked her seatbelt, not realizing that she would instantly fall on top of me due to the car now being on its side.

We managed to right ourselves; she was seriously shaken but appeared to be physically fine. I picked her up and lifted her towards the passenger window and she climbed out. I then climbed up to make my way out of the passenger window also, but by now the pain was overwhelming. As I pulled myself out of the window, I noticed that the impact of the crash had forced the glove compartment door to burst open and I could see a white carrier bag inside, concealing the cannabis I had just bought. By now loads of locals had gathered at the scene.

As I clambered from the car, I saw people embracing my girlfriend as she sobbed uncontrollably in their arms. The white summer dress she was wearing was almost completely red with the blood from my arms and hands. I looked down at my hand dripping with blood and felt like I was going to pass out from the pain; I had never felt anything like it before. I couldn't think straight, so I moved away from the crowd and laid down along the pavement. Closing my eyes, I could hear sirens approaching in the distance and the sound of people comforting my girlfriend. No one came to see if I was OK. No one seemed to care. I understood their concern for the girl, she was so obviously shaken, but inside my quiet exterior I was falling apart. I was injured and felt alone. I felt vulnerable. I felt helpless. All I needed was for someone to tell me that everything was going to be all right. But nobody did.

Reluctantly, I forced myself to sit up, but my body was so stiff and bruised it was difficult to move. Covered in blood, I opened my heavy eyes and looked around to get my bearings. To my surprise, I found myself sitting directly outside the entrance to a church. I couldn't believe it. The last couple of months had been among the most difficult months of my life, my only hope being found in little pockets of prayer. And now here I was, literally crashing and burning outside of a church. I was bloody and bruised and broken. I was so weak I couldn't register the significance of this moment. But as God often does, he was going to give me yet another chance to notice his presence.

The next thing I knew, I was surrounded by paramedics, the police and the fire brigade and then I was on a stretcher in the back of an ambulance and heading to hospital. On arrival, I was rushed into A&E where some receptionists quickly checked me in before I was taken through to a cubicle. As I lay waiting, I thought about the state I was in, literally covered in blood, with my right forearm full of puncture wounds from the glass. Then I remembered the cannabis.

I called out to one of the nurses, an Irish chap who seemed pretty cool, and asked him to find out if anyone had taken a bag out of the glove compartment of the car. He came back a short while later and informed me that unfortunately he hadn't managed to find anything out. I was left feeling anxious and restless as the condemnation started to kick in. Some police officers were floating around the hospital; every time I spotted one my stomach turned over as if I was on a fairground ride. How had I got myself into this mess? And more importantly, how was I going to get myself out of it?

All of a sudden, somebody pulled back the curtain to my cubicle, and my heart lurched before I saw who had just walked in – my mother. My heart filled with relief; my mother always had this way of making me feel as though everything was going to be all right, even when it wasn't. She didn't have to say a word; her presence alone was enough to help settle me down.

I had just finished explaining to her what had happened when a doctor entered the cubicle and explained to both of us that after looking at the X-rays, he felt the need to operate on my lower right arm due to glass fragments still lodged in there. I was so worried, but even more so when a police officer came into the cubicle to ask if he could have a word with me. The doctor didn't give me an opportunity to reply. He snapped at the officer, explaining that I had just been in a very serious crash and was about to have an operation. The officer looked fairly embarrassed and asked if it would be OK if he had a chat with me after the operation. I agreed. A nurse arrived shortly afterwards to prepare my arm for the operation. She cleaned the wounds up and I said goodbye to my mother before I got ushered to outside the operating theatre, where I lay on the bed in the empty corridor waiting for someone to take me in.

As I lay there, I wrestled with the condemnation filling my veins. I looked at the condition of my arms, my hands. I thought about the damage I had done to my car. I thought about the hurt I had caused my mother. I thought about the failure I had become. I had messed up big time this time.

Just then, I was disturbed by the gentle voice of an older nurse who appeared. She sounded of West Indian heritage. 'What's happened?' She had been walking past and stopped upon seeing my condition. She introduced herself and then gently asked me what my name was. I introduced myself and explained to her what had happened. Far from condemning me, she empathized with me. As we continued to talk for just a short moment longer, I felt my heart rate beginning to ease. The lady took a deep breath before asking the last question I was expecting.

'Claud, do you believe in God?'

I looked at her, knowing what she had asked me was serious. 'Yes,' I whispered. 'Yes, I do.'

'Good,' she smiled. 'You must believe in God. Can I tell you something?'

I nodded, wondering what she was going to say.

'I wasn't supposed to work tonight,' she said, looking into my eyes. 'I actually work at a different hospital, but this one called to ask whether I could come in and cover a shift. I didn't want to, but I said yes because I knew there was a reason that I was supposed to be here.' Each gentle word spoken in her warm voice echoed in my core. 'I was supposed to be here,' the nurse continued, 'because you and I were supposed to meet tonight, Claud. I know things have been difficult for you and you've been fighting for a long time.'

I remained silent, crippled with emotion.

'You see, there is a battle going on over your life,' her gentle voice explained. 'And you must turn to God.'

The tears trickled down my cheeks.

She leaned over and whispered in my ear, 'I'm going to give you my number and you must call me, Claud.'

I wiped away the tears and took the grey disposable hand towel that she had written her telephone number on. Before I knew it, she was gone. With only the tissue crushed into the ball of my fist to prove that I wasn't going mad, I lay there wondering what had just happened.

VERY SOON I REALIZED
THE SAME HABITS I
HAD FORMED IN MY
OLD NEIGHBOURHOOD
HAD FOLLOWED ME
TO MY NEW ONE.

CHAPTER NINE

How did I end up here? I asked myself the same question over and over in the days following the crash. My car was a write-off and my arm was in a sling, but worse than that, my pride was smashed to pieces. Despite the kind nurse's assurance that God was fighting for me, I still felt as if I was losing. I was losing my hard reputation and I was losing my hope. The condemnation I was living with was no longer simmering under the surface; it was at the forefront of my thoughts. How had the crash happened? Why hadn't the other car slowed down? Why did the driver run off? My girlfriend and I analysed every aspect of that day, just trying to understand.

Then I got a phone call that shocked me to my core. I was expecting to hear from the police, who had called to the house a number of times in the days following the crash. What I wasn't expecting was to be told by a solicitor that my girlfriend was intending to make some sort of compensation claim against me. I was lost for words. Not only did I adore the girl, but she had been alongside me every day since the crash. I had questioned her motives for being with me, but I never suspected that when she was asking me all those questions about the crash she'd simply been building her case against me. Like countless other people, she had never liked me for me. She had liked me for my reputation. And now that was in tatters, she wasn't going to stick around.

Though the girl's case was quickly thrown out of court, she still found other ways to hurt me. After we broke up, she went out of her way to meet up with some guys who she knew didn't like me and stir things up even more. I found myself feeling more vulnerable with each and every day that passed; I knew my enemies would carry their threats out if they got the opportunity to do so. I lay low at home, trying to figure out my next move, but it was hopeless. I had no transport, no work and no money. *We* had no money.

Though I should have known that my mother was struggling with money following my father's death, I was selfishly too wrapped up in my own affairs to understand the gravity of it until a few months after the crash, when she told me that we had to move to a new house. By now we had been in our house for ten years. I didn't want to leave, but we had no choice. Reluctantly, we packed up all of our belongings and moved to New Malden.

The emotional uprooting of moving to a new house again was even harder than the physical. So many memories from all of the years that we had spent there quickly came rushing back to me: thoughts of my father, his abuse, the police raids, my small bedroom, the place I ran to for shelter for so many years. I was leaving it all behind.

We arrived at the house in New Malden and began filling the rooms with the many boxes of our cheap possessions. I didn't know much about the area, but I secretly hoped that perhaps here I could make better choices than the ones I'd left behind. Shortly after our arrival, I managed to get a job working in a cinema that had just opened in Kingston. It was a great job and I got to watch loads of movies for free.

I particularly remember meeting loads of students who were only working at the cinema temporarily while studying, before they moved on to a better place in life. I had no better place; the cinema was my better place. For the first time in a long time, I felt good at something and I soon made friends with my colleagues, who would all join me at the pub after almost every shift. That's where I met Eddy.

Eddy was a tall Palestinian guy who absolutely loved to drink. Working at the cinema was meant to be my fresh start but, in many ways, I was still the same old me. Buzzing off this new social group, I soon started to get wasted with Eddy at every opportunity. Eddy was a little bit older than me and made me feel cool and accepted. So when he asked me whether I knew anyone who could get him some hash, I was desperate to please him. 'I can't get any hash . . .' I started. Eddy's face fell. 'But I can get us some amazing skunk.'

Very soon I realized the same habits I had formed in my old neighbourhood had followed me to my new one. That's the thing with bad habits. They are easy to form and really difficult to shake. I started becoming known in the bars around town, and once again I found myself playing up to the attention. We had a lot of fun nights out and I often blew my entire month's wage in the first week. That's how I ended up meeting Sarah.

In many ways, Sarah was the polar opposite to me. She was really cool and gentle, and spoke very well. Our birth date was perhaps the only thing we had in common. That and the fact that we seemed to like each other. I liked how she spoke, captivating listeners as she talked, including me.

She was educated and intended to study law at university. Hanging out with Sarah helped me to take my mind off of the state my life was really in. She made me feel that things might be getting better when they were anything but.

Where Sarah was a good influence, I was by now a bad one. I encouraged Eddy to smoke and drink more and more. He even came to his shifts with a bottle of water just to detox from the night before. Or so I thought. When Eddy was called into the manager's office and fired on the spot, I discovered it wasn't water in his bottle at work. It was vodka. We continued to hang out outside of work, but our time together was becoming less joyful, with Eddy's only interest seeming to be where he could purchase drugs. Distracted by my 'old' life, my new one at the cinema didn't seem to be a good fit any more. The managers were growing tired of my antics and I eventually got caught letting someone in to see a film for free and they politely asked me to leave.

Losing my job at the cinema was socially very embarrassing for me, and my new social life ended as quickly as it had begun. It seemed friends were people who were there when the party was happening, but long gone by the time real life resumed. Once again, I found myself falling into depression and despite no longer having an income, there was only one thing I knew I could rely on to make me feel better.

Sarah and I had continued to see one another through this time, but we both knew she was destined for better things and soon she was leaving for university. Deep down I always knew that it wouldn't last. No matter what I did, I always felt as though I wasn't good enough for her and I knew she could find someone much better than myself. I wasn't surprised when she told me that she had met someone shortly after leaving for university. I was, however, devastated. It wasn't just losing Sarah, although that was hard. It was that it was getting harder and harder to escape the reality of my situation. I spent most days locked away in my room, consuming as much cannabis as possible while single-handedly battling the millions of demons that had pursued me my whole life. No matter where I was, they followed me. Even so, when my mother told me we had to move house yet again, it still hurt. Moving so many times reminded me of the lack of stability in my life and this triggered an even deeper depression.

Depression was not new to me, but this time it felt different. It was deeper, darker and all-consuming, causing me to spend most of my days in reflection and self-pity, stumbling my way through the barrage of negative memories of what life had thrown at me over the years. I was drowning in anxiety, and panic attacks could strike at any time, leaving my heart racing at various times throughout each day. I would smoke more and more in the hope of escaping, but it only seemed to make things worse. I didn't want to smoke, but I couldn't find the strength to stop. I soon began to question everything. What was all this pain for? Was the hurting ever going to stop? Would life get any better than this? Was it even worth sticking around to find out?

Consumed by self-pity, I wasn't even thinking about God or what he wanted for me. Despite the times I had prayed and felt as though he was listening, I couldn't find any reason to hope. Things had always been financially difficult for my family, but by now my mother and I were living hand to mouth. We reached out to anyone we could for financial support but received no help. Having no access to the internet, I would look in the local newspaper for jobs, but they were few and far between. Those that were available, I didn't have experience in or wasn't qualified for, which at the time felt like just another reminder that I wasn't good enough at anything. We soon reached a level of poverty that I hadn't experienced before, living off bread, milk, tea and potatoes; we had bread and butter sandwiches for lunch and dinner for weeks. I used to scurry back from buying these basic provisions, hoping not to bump into anyone I knew en route. Such was the shame of our situation. I was now 21 years of age and wasn't able to provide for my mother. Even worse, I felt like a burden to her. How had I gone from street star to barely being able to afford bread? And without any qualifications or the sort of skills needed to be able to get some, how was it going to get better?

One day, after I had finished counting out pennies from the penny jar, I made my way to the newsagent's to get a cheap bag of potatoes. On the way, I heard someone yelling from a passing car, which seemed to be moving alongside me in a long line of traffic leading up to the main road. At first I ignored the yelling and continued on my way, but as the traffic moved on the car got closer to me. I realized that someone seemed to be desperately trying to get my attention. When the driver started beeping his horn, I looked around and was surprised to see Eddy sitting behind the wheel. I smiled and raised my hand to wave, but before I could, Eddy quickly pulled the car over, cutting me off on the pavement. I greeted him with a handshake and asked him how he was, even though he looked awful.

'Claud,' he said, ignoring my question completely. 'Can you get any hash?'

'No,' I said cautiously, but then remembering that I was on my way to buy the cheapest packet of potatoes with just about the only money we had, I added, 'But I can get some cannabis?'

Eddy keenly agreed and we exchanged numbers before parting company. On the way home from the newsagent's, I felt an excitement in the pit of my stomach. For the first time in a long time my imagination came alive with possibility. On some level I knew drugs were responsible for so many of my issues, but on another I felt I had no choice. I was so tired of feeling hungry.

By the time I got home my heart was racing and my hands were shaking with excitement. Putting the potatoes on the kitchen counter, I explained to my mother what had just happened. She couldn't understand why I'd be excited about it. But then I explained the formula to her; that we would be able to afford to eat properly again. The only problem was that I needed some money to buy the drugs to sell on in the first place.

'Do you have any . . .' I began to ask my mother before thinking better of it. I already knew she had nothing more than the £40 that would have to see us through the week. I promised her that I'd make everything work out. I knew that I had to.

I raised the remaining £5 that I needed by emptying the rest of the money from the penny jar that sat on our kitchen counter. Then my mother and I drove to Croydon and after waiting around for a good while, I finally met with my contact. I made my way back to our car and got in, the skunk so potent that its powerful smell quickly filled the small car. My mother instinctively reached across and opened her window about two inches – just enough room to allow the cold fresh air to burst in from outside. I was acting on my instincts too.

It was dark when we arrived home and by now Eddy was calling every half an hour, his desperation growing with each and every call. We were desperate too. This wasn't the first time I had bought drugs, nor was it the largest amount, but it was definitely the most important drug deal I had ever been involved with. All of a sudden, the stakes were higher as the reality of our situation kicked in; everything was riding on this. I had stopped caring about my own well-being long ago. I was doing this for my mother.

Mind racing, I took the cannabis into my bedroom and weighed it up with the old set of digital scales I had previously inherited from one of my brothers. Eddy was already waiting for me by the time I arrived at our arranged meeting place. When I handed Eddy's bundle over to him, he asked whether we could meet again the next day, but this time I was to bring two. Walking away, euphoria filled my veins. On the way back from meeting Eddy the next day, I randomly bumped into Phil, my old school friend who still lived locally. It didn't take long for Phil to ask me whether I could get him any drugs. We exchanged numbers.

By the time I arrived home my excitement was almost uncontainable. I got ready for bed and tried to settle down to sleep, but my imagination was running wild with thoughts about how much money I would make for me and my mother, and how my life was going to change as a result. Somehow, I'd managed to remember all the perks attached to my life of crime without being able to recall the underlying pain. Either way, I felt I had no choice. I had spent the last couple of years in the depths of depression, reaching rock bottom. Now I just wanted us to be back on top. I wanted the rush of euphoria that comes from a drug deal. I wanted my notoriety back. I wanted to lie awake at night just counting down to the next deal, where every second that passed felt like a second closer to being immortalized. I was ready for it all. And why wouldn't I be? I had been preparing for it my whole life.

EVERY PERSON I
SUPPLIED DRUGS
TO HAD THEIR OWN
STORY, AND THOUGH
DRUGS MADE LIFE
SEEM BETTER FOR
A MOMENT, THERE
ALWAYS CAME A
POINT WHERE THEY
WOULD SPELL AN
UNHAPPY ENDING.

CHAPTER TEN

In the beginning, I simply wanted to make enough money to enable my mother and me to put food on the table, but before long my thirst for financial gain started to grow again. Perhaps it was inevitable. The more money I began to turn over, the more money I began to want. Next, I wanted enough money to buy a moderate car and told myself that I would be content with just that. Then I wanted a better car and told myself the same. The contentment never came. I know now that the apostle Paul calls us to be 'content whatever the circumstances', saying that he had 'learned the secret of being content in any and every situation, whether well fed or hungry, whether living in plenty or in want' (Philippians 4.11–12). But Paul had Jesus, and at this time I felt further from God than ever before. All I wanted was *more*.

As time passed, my small business began to grow, and with it my interest for growing my small business. With my moral compass well and truly bent, I soon developed an obsession for 'the hustle' that was taking over my life. In the same way I had become consumed with my Brian Greenaway obsession or my football obsession, I started to fill in all of my gaps with the one thing I thought I was good at. I would read anything I could get my hands on that was related to growing a business. I was fascinated with the industry and even enrolled in a short business studies course at a local college. Once a week, I would go along to a local evening class and we discussed strategies and margins. Nobody knew that my particular business idea was far from legit.

I bought DVDs about notorious gangsters and watched these movies late into the night, imagining implementing their success strategies into my own personal approach. If I wasn't watching movies, I was reading books, studying the Godfather and his mafia family in Italy. I was so caught up in the life I had created for myself that I barely took any time to consider the consequences of what I was actually doing. All of the stories and movies were just that – *stories*, a form of entertainment with actors playing a role. They were not meant to be imitated and duplicated. At the end of every book I read, the criminal got caught and went to prison, or worse. By now, however, my stupidity had taken such a hold of me that I couldn't see the warning signs. It wasn't as if I was even the one taking the drugs. I guess the drug for me was selling them. Building my reputation. Making money. Making something of myself.

I had grown so selfish and greedy that I would sell practically anything to anyone. The limitations that I once set for myself were by now obliterated. Although I had started out by selling cigarettes at school and then cannabis from the garage, as I was nearing my late twenties my catalogue of products and customers had grown exponentially. I now sold to people of all sorts of backgrounds from all different places. As my notoriety grew, so did my network. I didn't care who I was selling to provided I was selling.

For example, I remember a homeless chap up in Piccadilly Circus who spent his days begging and whenever he had made enough to score, he would arrange to meet me. I would watch him as he got off the floor and climbed into the back of my car, ready to hand over his carrier bag full of coins. The thought of it is so far from what I now know about how Jesus tells us to care for the poor, it reminds me just how obsessed with the pursuit of wealth and notoriety I had become. And yet, before things got better – better than I could ever imagine – they were about to get worse.

I received a phone call from a man who had got my number from a mutual 'friend'. Though I previously wouldn't have gone to meet a random individual, by this point I didn't really care; after speaking briefly, we made arrangements to meet at his flat. Arriving at the local council estate he lived on, I walked towards his flat, stalling at the condition of the front garden. The bushes were overgrown, allowing very little light into the garden. The front gate was missing and there were empty cans and all sorts of other rubbish scattered everywhere. As I discreetly looked around, I noticed that the dirty stained curtains on the windows were still drawn and I couldn't help but wonder when they had last been opened. Standing there in the front garden, I could feel eyes on me. I felt deeply uneasy, but then that was nothing new. These surrounding signs of neglect weren't uncommon at the places and premises that I would visit. Failing to locate a bell, I reached up and knocked on the front door, which opened quickly but cautiously.

As a hand rested on the door frame, I noticed the dark, heavy build-up of dirt under the fingernails. Our eyes locked on one another and he gave me a nod.

'I'm Steve,' he said, using his head to direct me to step in. As Steve turned around to lead the way, I noticed a number of tattoos on his arms, including the bold letters HMP tattooed on the top of his right arm. Following him into the house, I was greeted by the exposed grey concrete floor running throughout the house, and my initial concerns quickly started to increase. Moving further into the house, we came to two wooden doors, the left leading to the kitchen and the right leading to the front room. Both doors had holes in them – fist-sized holes. I followed Steve through the door on the right, and he steered me into a front room where there was a makeshift bed on the floor in front of the main window, surrounded by beer cans everywhere. The place was a mess and the smell matched the condition of the place. I tried to hold my breath in between sentences.

As Steve talked, spitting while he did, I felt very aware of him stepping around me to close the door into the room. My heart started to beat faster as I tried to gauge his intentions; being set up or robbed was commonplace in this underhand industry. I mentally started sizing him up. He looked as though he had had a hard life and was easily ten years older than myself; I reasoned that if need be, I could take him. A few more moments passed, then the door across the living room slowly opened. I watched in surprise as an extremely overweight figure squeezed himself through the doorway and into the room. Steve broke the awkward silence by introducing the man to me as Smithy.

Smithy was an ox of a man, no taller than 5 foot 8 and weighing at least 35 stone, he had a skinhead and tattoos all over his body. After making his way across the small living room, he slumped unashamedly on to the couch, struggling to catch his breath. I proceeded to introduce myself, pretending not to notice his body mass. I'm not sure if Smithy intentionally wore a really small pair of spectacles to achieve a 'Charles Bronson' effect, or if it was actually just the size of his head that made his glasses look so small. Either way, they complemented his menacing look perfectly. My eyes read the tattoos on his body like a magazine as he sat there bare-chested and panting. That's when I noticed the rather intimidating giant St George's shield tattooed across his gut and the initials NF tattooed just above the thumb of his right hand. National Front? My heart started to race. To make matters worse, Smithy stirred to reveal a couple of Nazi signs tattooed on his arms.

I knew then that the situation could escalate quickly if I wasn't careful. Every racially motivated attack in any film or programme I had ever seen flashed through my mind. Heart racing, I came to the realization that these guys were real NF skinheads and I wouldn't be able to fight both of them on my own. Neither of them had yet shown any signs of intending to pay me for their order, so I presumed that they were going to rob me, but I knew I had to stay strong.

'All right, fellas,' I said, trying to hide any uncertainty in my voice. 'Who's going to pay me for this?' I reached down to pull out the order from the pocket of my jeans. After a moment that stretched for miles, Smithy reached to give me the money and, handing over the product, I raced out of there as soon as I could.

As with so many things in my life, I wish I could say this dangerous moment was a turning point for me, but whatever fear I felt was always outweighed by my desire for more. I reasoned I was too far in to turn back now. Before long, Steve and Smithy had become friends, or at least as close to friends as a mixed-raced drug dealer could be with two white skinheads from the National Front. The three of us talked a lot during my visits, to the point where I felt comfortable enough to ask about their racist tattoos. Taking the time to listen to their background, I realized that Steve and Smithy's issues with race were more of a statement than an actual belief. They were good guys at heart, who had had incredibly difficult lives. I soon discovered that they had first met while in foster care as children and had both spent most of their adult lives in and out of prison, where they'd had to learn how to fight to survive – and also got their tattoos. When you are in a minority you feel weak, and that was something I could relate to. Like me, Steve and Smithy were looking for something to relate to, but we were all looking in the wrong places.

I remember arriving at the estate once and as I walked up towards the house Steve excitedly stuck his head out of the window and shouted, 'Here comes the poisoner!' Soon, the name stuck. At the time I thought of it as harmless fun, but all that was about to change. Smithy started to call me when Steve was at work; he wanted to buy gear that he wouldn't have to share. When I did go around to see him alone, Smithy always took a long time to answer the front door and when he finally did, he was always out of breath. His weight was a real issue for him. I imagine he had suffered with weight issues his whole life, but it didn't stop him from buying a lot of drugs. At first, I was reluctant to sell him so much product, but I was so clouded by darkness that I thought: *What's the worst that can happen?*

One day, I received a phone call out of the blue from a lady who would often stay with Smithy. She lived on the same estate and suffered from some sort of schizophrenia, but she and Smithy had become firm friends. Answering the phone, I heard her crying: 'Hello? Hello? I don't know what to do!'

At first I wondered whether she was out of it. I asked her to slow down. 'What's the problem?' I said.

'It's Smithy,' she cried, as my heart stopped. 'He's not moving. Shall I call an ambulance? I've called an ambulance. What shall I do?' she rambled on at speed.

I explained to her as slowly as I could that first she needed to wait for the ambulance to arrive and secondly, she needed to promise that she would never tell anyone that she and I had spoken. *Ever.* I didn't know what was wrong with Smithy, but I was very aware that there might be drugs and packaging on the scene that could lead back to me. As soon as the call ended, I switched my mobile off, drove as far across town as I could and put it in a public bin. I was scared and wanted to distance myself from everything immediately. A few days later, I received a call on my new number. It was Steve.

'Smithy died from a heart attack.' He explained the series of events that had led to his death; I could hear the emotion and despair in his voice. As I listened to him speak, my stomach churned. How much had I contributed to Smithy's heart attack? He was a 35-stone man, snorting fairly large quantities of drugs on a daily basis; it was never going to end well. I should have known my actions were adversely affecting his health, but at the time I didn't even think about it. I was only looking out for myself, and for me all that mattered was making money. Long before I knew Jesus died for me, my actions were killing others.

Every person I supplied drugs to had their own story, and though drugs made life seem better for a moment, there always came a point where they would spell an unhappy ending. There was another chap I had come to know well who had unfortunately started using cocaine when he was in his early teens. Sadly, this had developed into a lifelong addiction. He was older than me, had children and had been with their mother for many years. They all lived in a flat together and he sold drugs mainly to supply his and his partner's habit, which is often the case. Unfortunately, this chap had been diagnosed with sickle cell disease at a very young age, which meant he was often in and out of hospital.

One day, I got a call from him to say he was in hospital, which was no real surprise; what did surprise me, however, was that this time he was asking me to deliver drugs to him there. I told him that I didn't think it was a good idea, but he insisted and I was weak. After all, what did I have to lose? We arranged to meet around the back of the hospital by the car park, out of view, and agreed that I would park my car a few roads away and walk to the hospital so as to avoid any suspicion.

Within a few minutes of my arriving, he came to meet me as planned, but to my surprise he was being pushed in a wheelchair by his girlfriend. I couldn't believe my eyes, as just 24 hours earlier I had seen him and he appeared to be fine. Now here he was, bloated and swollen and unable to walk. He reassured me that everything was going to be fine and that the drugs would help, so we met for the next few days.

Then I got a call from his girlfriend. I assumed she was calling to arrange another pick-up for him, but she broke down. Through sobs she explained that my friend had died due to organ failure. I listened silently while she explained that the doctors still wanted to do an autopsy, as they needed to confirm what the cause of death was. As she did, her tone changed. Was she accusing me? Was she implying that his death was my fault? Looking back, I can see that my behaviour was making matters infinitely worse. At the time, though, the feelings of shame and depression that I couldn't even articulate only pushed me further down my road of demolition and destruction; things had always been bad, but now they were out of control.

It wasn't just my clients whose lives were being destroyed by drug taking; it was also my friends – friends I had grown up with, like Phil. We had once had so much fun escaping the world together. Now, the very means we had used to escape were making the world an infinitely more difficult place. By now, Phil had developed an aggressive cocaine addiction and our friendship was turning into a relationship of creditor and debtor. I remember one evening Phil met with me to make a collection and as he stood before me, one of my closest friends in the world, his face started to change. Rubbing his chest frantically, Phil started to moan; his heart was beating too fast. He told me he would be fine and urged me to carry on with the deal, but I found out a few days later that he had ended up in hospital that night.

The drugs weren't fun any more. Now, we were desperate. Even my friend Eddy from the cinema, once the best fun to be around, knew the party was over. His recreational usage had changed into a dangerous addiction and I had begun to notice his erratic behaviour. He would go missing for a while every few months and then reappear with a huge amount of money to spend. I later found out that he had at some point been sectioned and when he disappeared, he would be in hospital getting clean. As soon as he was clean and released to his parents' house, he would make his way straight to me and reload again. Eddy wasn't the only one I took advantage of; there were many others over the years. And even though I thought I was benefiting, I didn't realize the toll it was taking on my soul.

A death in a business can be the death of a business. But more than that, you can feel a bit of yourself die with it. I thought I had been preparing to be a drug dealer my whole life – it was the only thing I was ever good at – but nothing could have prepared me for that. All the gangster movies in the world couldn't prepare me for the harsh reality of death. I was sure that people knew the bad news that had been following me around, but it's the kind of thing that nobody wants to admit, so it just goes unsaid. But I still noticed the reaction. The silence for the first few weeks after a death was almost unbearable. People distanced themselves, and though nobody was saying anything to my face, I knew it was because everything was being said behind my back. It's the kind of thing that gives you nightmares, that you think about before you go to sleep at night and first thing when you wake up, haunting your every thought. In destroying so many other people's lives, I had destroyed my own. I knew I needed saving, rescuing, something to hope for, a hand to hold on to. Just when I was praying silently in youth club and feeling something shift, I needed connection. And yet with all my bridges well and truly burnt, only detachment remained.

It takes a different level of detachment to deal with a death and it wasn't like people respected you in my line of work for showing any emotion. I reminded myself of the basics time and time again: *never show emotion or weakness, always hide your fears. Never appear to be vulnerable, as opportunists are always waiting to strike. Trust no one, friend or foe.* It was a lonely lifestyle to live. I thought the only way to get over it was to own it, but I struggled to do so as the reality of my situation became apparent like never before.

I felt that life had smacked me in the mouth. The death and injury count among my clients was soaring and though I hadn't been directly responsible for the deaths, there was no doubt that I had helped contribute towards them. I had seen all sorts of people succumb to the dangers of drugs. Smart, working people; actors you have seen on television; the most beautiful women offering sexual favours in return for their next hit.

I only ever accepted cash. That was my fix. After a lifetime of having little, I always wanted a lot, and now, with the trauma of losing clients heavy on my heart, I tried to shop myself happy. When I went shopping, I would always carry lots of cash so that I could buy anything that caught my eye, from designer clothes to cars. I often found myself mooching around expensive department stores just to have the staff there call me Mr Jackson. My ego was so fragile, it depended on it. I also depended on the affirmation of women and began dating multiple women at the same time. It was just my latest way of not taking any responsibility for my behaviour. Back then, I never knew what accountability was; all I was concerned about was escaping the dark cloud that had been looming over my head for most of my life. No matter how much I spent or what I bought, deep down I was never really happy. Something was still missing and I couldn't understand it.

I had long exceeded my eldest brother's financial success. In fact, I was the most financially successful person in my entire family by a long shot. At some point or other every family member had come to me for money, but soon it started to cause a divide. I grew very paranoid and began not to trust anyone, friends or family. That's what happens when you treat others badly: you start to believe they'll treat you the same in return. Perhaps one of the best-known proverbs in the Bible is 'do to others what you would have them do to you' (Matthew 7.12). I was doing bad things to others and so expected bad treatment in return. I started to worry that the women in my life would find out I was unfaithful. I started to worry that certain family members were trying to con me out of money. I started to worry about losing more clients, about more and more friends being killed due to knife and gun crime. All of the peers I had looked up to when I was younger were mostly in prison. I had every reason to be paranoid. And I knew I had to do something to protect myself before it was too late.

I HAD NO IDEA THEN THAT I WAS ABOUT TO BECOME BOTH STRONGER AND MORE VULNERABLE THAN I'D EVER BEEN IN MY LIFE.

CHAPTER ELEVEN

To be protected has meant many things throughout the course of my life. When I was small, it meant being embraced by my mother or trained to box by my brothers. When I was older, it meant having a reputation that won me friends, and friends who kept my reputation on top. By the age of 30, and with so many bridges burned, protection had to mean something else. With paranoia clouding my every thought, I knew I needed some legitimate work to cover the tracks left by what was now 15 years of illegitimate business.

It was around this time that an opportunity arose for me to volunteer within my local council, mentoring high-risk young offenders. I knew a chap who worked for the council and I would see him around locally, so it wasn't a surprise to bump into him one day – what was a surprise was what he said next: 'We're looking for a mentor. You'd be awesome.' I walked away, warmed by the compliment but confused nonetheless.

Soon after that, for some reason I was looking through the local newspaper and I saw the volunteering opportunity the guy from the council had told me about. The role seemed simple, consisting of supervising the young people while they were completing their reparation orders. I never imagined I'd enjoy being a mentor when I first agreed to do the role – I just knew it was a great cover-up. Who would possibly believe that one of the mentors working for the council was a drug dealer in his spare time? It was perfect. Looking back now, however, I think there was also some kind of secret desire hidden within me to make a difference.

Things started really well and before long I was offered a position as a paid sessional worker and granted my own pass and council ID card, which I wore around my neck with pride. I remember on one occasion getting pulled over in my car for speeding and, with the ID around my neck, I stepped out of the car before the police officers could get out of theirs. This was something I would often do when pulled over, as it would give off the impression that I had nothing to hide. When they started to question me on this occasion, it soon came up that I was a mentor for high-risk young offenders with the local council. All of a sudden, the tone of our conversation seemed to change, and the officers began to show genuine interest. Before long, they were joking about how they were surprised I wasn't driving faster in such a beautiful car! After chatting for a few more seconds we shook hands and parted ways. I couldn't believe what had just happened; they didn't even search my car. Up until this point, the law had been the enemy to me and my peers. Now, with my legitimate role, I felt I had more power. I had no idea then that I was about to become both stronger and more vulnerable than I'd ever been in my life.

I found it surprising that my cover-up was working so well, but what surprised me more was the fact that I was actually enjoying it. I met some great people while working for the council. I was asked into meetings and for some reason my opinion appeared to count for something. While there, I created behavioural programmes and implemented them within the sector that I was working in. I had trouble-some young men with serious reputations filling out feedback forms and providing a whole new insight into their behavioural patterns. No one else could get the guys to cooperate, but the more time I spent with them, the more I found myself relating to some of the individuals. Many of them hadn't had the best start in life and neither had I. Speaking to them, I cast my mind back to the times when I was a child facing poverty with my family. I thought about when the teachers would segregate me in school and I was made to sit on my own for hours in halls and corridors. I thought about my teenage years, and later, when my mother and I had only bread to eat. Mentoring those young men, I often wondered whether I might even be making a positive impact on them. And yet, when I left for home at the end of the working day, the dark realities of my life would quickly return to haunt me and I would revert to my typical mind-set. I had developed a love–hate relationship with myself and with life. I loved what I had achieved but hated what I had become. I loved what I was doing through mentoring, but I hated that it still wasn't enough to make me give up the drugs game I had spent most of my life playing. All that was about to change, however.

A few weeks into working for the council, I met a man called Pete. Pete was my manager's manager's manager, and was more or less the head of an entire department within the council. We were nothing alike. Where I was loud, always with a point to prove, Pete was polite, calm and unflustered. Where I would lean back in my office chair with my designer clothes on, Pete would sit upright, typing away in his white button-up shirt. Where I'd go out and pay for lunch every day, Pete wore a backpack and brought a packed lunch with him. And where I'd drive one of my cars into work each day and pay for parking, even though I lived within walking distance of the offices, Pete would catch public transport. I often found myself looking across the office at him, just trying to work him out. What kind of man was he? Why was he so kind? Then one day I got my chance to find out.

Logging on to my computer one day, I got an email informing me of a team-building day that I simply couldn't avoid. Everybody from every department of the office was required to take part, so I reluctantly went along. One by one we all had to take turns in an 'ice breaker', which consisted of each of us standing up to introduce ourselves and share something that no one else knew about us. Everybody nervously took their turn and as they did, I realized that I was waiting for Pete to have his go. By now, I had tried to upstage him many times in the office and couldn't; no matter who was around, Pete would always say good morning to me when he saw me. Nobody else had really bothered before.

Finally, it was Pete's turn to stand up. As I sat there on the edge of my seat I was sure he was going to declare that he collected toy trains or still played with Star Wars figurines – both of which would have been fine – but then the strangest thing happened. He reached down into his pocket and took out a tiny little black ring box, which he held gently in his hands before opening it. The entire room was silent; you could have literally heard a pin drop. Reaching into the box,

Pete held up a small crucifix between thumb and forefinger. Lifting the cross high into the air, he said, 'Hi, my name's Pete, and I'm a Christian.'

I looked on, completely awestruck. I couldn't believe it. For some reason, I found myself feeling completely overwhelmed, like I had been hit right between the eyes with a lightning bolt. Pete continued to speak about Jesus and how he had changed his life, but I didn't hear a word he was saying. I was still trying to get my head around it all and couldn't take my eyes off the crucifix that he was holding. I watched on as the polite, quiet man I had disregarded countless times before stood there with a certain vulnerability, bearing all of his insecurities to the world. I realized then that above and beyond drug dealers and professional criminals, Pete was actually one of the bravest people I had ever encountered in my life. I was convicted by his conviction. His beautiful boldness was like nothing I had ever seen. That's when it hit me. Pete had nothing that I had and everything that I wanted.

Of all the things I had seen and encountered, this moment was my turning point. Not visiting my brother in prison. Not flipping my car, and my encounter with the kind nurse that night. Not even dealing drugs to someone who died of a heart attack shortly after. No, this simple man with his quiet demeanour, speaking from the heart, changed everything. In that moment, I realized I had spent my whole life fighting to prove my point. Fighting demon after demon, I had fixed my attention on accumulating as much money as I could, even if it meant losing my freedom or possibly even my life in the process. I had driven myself to the edge of madness, trying to prove my intelligence. And all to convince myself I wasn't worthless.

Sitting there in that small room, I wondered where Pete had got his boldness from. Hundreds of thousands of pounds had passed through my hands over the years, but I didn't have the boldness or the satisfaction that seemed to ooze from him. All of the money in the world couldn't buy his gentle confidence or security. I'd had so many girlfriends, but had never found love. My reputation was far greater than I was, but I still lived in fear. I had achieved everything that I'd wanted to, but still lacked inner fulfilment. The more I thought about it, the more intrigued I became. I reasoned that if Christianity was what fuelled Pete, then surely I needed to find out more about Christianity. Once again, I found myself asking the question: *What have I got to lose?*

There was no doubt about it, I just had to speak with Pete. After the event, he had to shoot off, as he had a train to catch, but I knew I couldn't miss this opportunity to speak to him. I asked if I could give him a lift to the station, but he politely declined my offer; he was more than happy to walk, as it wasn't far. I refused to take no for an answer, and though he technically had the power to get me fired, I insisted that he allow me to give him a lift to the station. Eventually he gave in.

While en route in the car, I spared him the small talk and immediately asked about his testimony. I explained that I was feeling moved by what I had heard him share with the group and wanted to know how I could learn more. He asked if I had ever heard of an Alpha course, and briefly explained to me that the Alpha course seeks to introduce the basics of Christian faith through a series of talks and discussions. It is described by its organizers as an opportunity to explore the 'meaning of life', and after trying to find it in so many different and dark places, I was ready to try anything to discover the light that Pete was carrying.

After dropping him off, I sped home and researched the Alpha course online. To my surprise there was a course starting the very next day. I immediately sent an email off to the organizers, asking if I could enrol on the course. I was worried that I would be too late.

The following morning, I could barely contain my excitement when I received a very warm email from a member of the Alpha team called Sharon, confirming my place on the course: 'We would be delighted if you could join us for Alpha this term!' I read the email again and again. I couldn't believe what I was reading. Sharon said that they would be *delighted* if I could join them this term. I found myself filling with excitement over something other than drugs and money for the first time in years. It reminded me of the time I had first heard Brian Greenaway speak or had prayed to God in prison. But somehow this time I knew things would be different. I *needed* them to be different.

The rest of my day went as routinely as it normally did. I got ready and went to the gym and by about midday my 'work' phone was starting to ring. Clients were waking up and looking for their next fix. I would normally try to coordinate delivery times around my work for the council, as I knew better than to take any product with me into the office. This day, however, it wasn't my phone holding my attention. It was the clock; the hands couldn't go round quickly enough. I just couldn't wait to get to the Alpha course!

The course was hosted by a very small church in west London, but thankfully for me was held in a cool independent coffee shop opposite the church. The cosy space was filled with jars and jars of coffee, with homemade tarts and the likes on the menu. I was nervous going into such an unknown setting, but at least it wasn't a traditional church, and I decided that since several people had tried to stab me in the past, the Alpha course had to be a piece of cake compared to the rest of my life.

On arrival I was welcomed by an American lady who introduced herself to me as Sharon, the woman who had emailed me. Sharon was a super-cool lady, slightly older than me and filled with kindness and sincerity. She introduced me to her husband Aaron, whose great sense of humour was complemented by his warm demeanour. Sharon then introduced me to the other Alpha team members, Bill and Lou. I remember being taken aback by how young Bill and Lou seemed to be when Bill introduced Lou to me as his wife. They were a great couple. Lou was super-intelligent, with a truckload of passion, and I enjoyed conversing with her very much; our dialogue was always filled with encouraging and thought-provoking discussion. Bill was basically everything I had always wanted to be. He was charming, well spoken and boy-band good-looking, not to mention he had this ability to hold a good conversation with anyone about anything. Like Sharon and her husband,

Bill and Lou had a great way of making individuals feel welcome and valued.

There were a number of individuals from all sorts of backgrounds and areas taking part in the Alpha course. The evening started well and the atmosphere in the room was amazing as we all chatted over a great meal. We then went on to watch a short talk that explored Christianity in an easy digestible format. After the talk, we were separated into small groups and invited to discuss and explore what we had just seen. The chats were lively and exciting; everyone had questions to ask and all of them were welcomed. I couldn't believe the buzz that could be achieved from simply being with people, and as the session drew to an end, I was already thinking about coming back.

I woke up the next day very reflective of the night before. Any attempts to plan my day ahead were unsuccessful. All I could think about was the Alpha course and what the following week was going to be like. I had lots of questions that I wanted answers to and as much as I had enjoyed the first session, I knew I wanted more. I always wanted more. Whether it was money or girls or cars or notoriety. But this time, I couldn't help wondering whether maybe wanting more was a *good* thing.

Despite the tiny flicker of hope inside me, I couldn't deny the fact that nothing in my life had really changed. I was still an empty cold-hearted drug dealer who lacked self-worth and confidence. I was still a poisoner whose only interest and focus was purely financial gain. In the week following the first Alpha session, I began to convince myself that I was just going along for the sake of it and I told myself that I would take part in the course for the social aspect if nothing else. Little did I know that God had other plans.

It was soon time for the second session, and on arrival I was met by Sharon and Lou at the entrance. I naturally reached out to greet Sharon with a handshake but was surprisingly welcomed with a huge hug! I was caught off guard, not used to people being so welcoming towards me. As Sharon and I hugged, I looked over at Lou and she cheerfully giggled, and I felt my cold, rugged heart beat so hard I thought it was going to jump right up out of the collar of my T-shirt. These people were clearly not like me.

As I entered the room and greeted everyone, I was approached by Bill. He had a huge smile on his face and seemed genuinely pleased to see me. Before I could say anything, he opened his arms and gave me a huge hug. I tried my best to hide my embarrassment, but I just didn't know what to do or how to respond; it was the first time I could remember another male giving me a hug. My family didn't do things like that, I didn't even hug my brothers, and here was Bill hugging me in public. I felt slightly emotional, but quickly composed myself, all the while surprised that the evening had started just as well as the last.

As I sat attentively listening, soaking up the atmosphere like a slice of bread in a bowl of soup, I felt the last shreds of my cynicism slipping away. Part of me had come along thinking, *What could these Christian folk possibly teach me?*, but as we discussed the short talk that we had watched at the beginning of the session, all of their points seemed reasonable. For the first time in a long time I trusted the people in front of me.

Week three quickly rolled around and I had spent the whole week thinking about everything we had discussed so far. Of all that I had seen and heard, though, one thing stood out among them all: I was really struck by how Bill, Lou, Sharon and Aaron spoke about Jesus. Even though I had had spiritual encounters and a chequered relationship with God, I hadn't really ever heard of Jesus – let alone been around Christians! Until now, the only things I'd heard about Jesus seemed like some sort of myth, or at best an old folk tale. But Bill, Lou, Sharon and Aaron spoke about Jesus confidently, as if Jesus actually existed. More than that, they talked as though somehow they knew him personally.

It was at this point in my journey with Alpha that the course took a vital turn. As usual, after eating our food, the team put on a DVD, which showed a short talk exploring Christianity. This talk felt different; it was less exploratory and more encouraging, and as it drew to an end, it offered the opportunity for individuals to personally invite Jesus into their lives. I knew this was it. I felt it was time to put my money where my mouth was. I knew that if I was to invite Jesus into my life, I would have to see a change in me; I wasn't prepared to pretend to be a happy-go-lucky Christian. I'd spent my entire existence gambling with my life, going against the odds, and I wasn't going to change now. If I was going to invite Jesus into my life, I was going all in. *Go big or go home,* I thought as I closed my eyes and took a deep breath. I had never been more serious about anything in my entire life. I needed this. I needed Jesus.

The atmosphere was incredible as people bowed their heads and began to pray. It was so quiet; I could literally feel the silence. It was right there and then that I laid all my cards on the table. In the intimacy of the moment, I welcomed Jesus into my life. And though my lips may have welcomed Jesus, my heart *dared* him. My heart dared him to come into my life and make a change. I needed him to make a change. I had taken so many wrong turns and climbed so many ladders that led nowhere. I was broken and bruised and disappointed. After spending the best part of a decade building my drug-dealing empire, I didn't want any of it. It wasn't what I wanted to do with the rest of my life. I needed Jesus to change things.

Little did I know then that the change would begin to happen almost immediately. Deep down, I felt my invite had been received. A short while later the group leader closed in prayer and my attention drifted back into the room. As I opened my eyes, I strangely felt at peace. I looked around at all of the great people I had met so far and felt a deep joy within myself that I hadn't felt in a really long time, maybe even ever.

The next few weeks consisted of a lot of thought and reflection. Day after day, week after week, I was growing extremely aware of my actions and intent. Unlike previous encounters I had had with God, which would come quickly and fade away, this time the change remained. I had become all too aware of what I had been doing to make a living and the fact that it wasn't actually all right. I was no longer OK with it and I knew I never would be.

I wasn't just selling drugs; I was in actual fact poisoning people and profiting from it. I was failing a society that had failed me, directly helping to destroy my community. I was taking advantage of vulnerable individuals who needed help. Individuals who needed love, not drugs. The very same people I claimed to be able to relate to and love: the underdogs, the have-nots, the outcasts, the rejected. As I learnt about a Jesus who cared for the least, the last and the lost, I couldn't ignore the reality of the harm I was doing. I could no longer escape or deny the responsibility of my actions, nor did I want to.

As the Alpha course continued, my feelings became more apparent and present. The Christians I had met confirmed my thoughts, not in word but in action. I had changed in my heart; my purpose was no longer to profit. In Matthew 10 in the Bible, Jesus is recorded as saying: 'Whoever finds their life will lose it, and whoever loses their life for my sake will find it' (verse 38). Now I wanted to give up my life, give up everything, so I could truly find myself. I knew the change in me couldn't remain by my own strength. I knew I had to do something. I could no longer continue to live the way I had been. I knew it was time to come clean.

YET MY DESIRE TO
SEEK REPENTANCE
AND PURSUE JESUS
WAS FAR GREATER
THAN MY FEAR OF
WHAT MIGHT HAPPEN
TO ME AS A RESULT OF
SPEAKING OUT.

CHAPTER TWELVE

The first time I encountered the Holy Spirit I didn't know what was happening, but shortly after inviting Jesus into my life, I definitely felt moved by something greater than myself. It was for that reason I found myself en route to meet the vicar of the church where I had just completed the Alpha course, to come clean about my life of crime.

I knew it was time to tell someone about the way I was living, to bring so much of what had happened in darkness into the light. I didn't know anything about the Church or vicars at the time but knew that people were always confessing their sins to vicars in movies, so it seemed like the right thing to do. We arranged to meet in a pub close to the church and I remember that with every step I took in his direction, my anxiety started to rise. I had spent my whole life being conditioned to never tell anyone anything. From the things I witnessed at home as a child to the way I made my money as an adult, I was taught never to speak of the heinous things I had done or seen. Yet my desire to seek repentance and pursue Jesus was far greater than my fear of what might happen to me as a result of speaking out.

Walking into the pub, I saw the vicar sitting there. To my naive eyes, he was a vicar in every sense of the word: nice, reserved, introverted, happy-go-lucky. I remember thinking that he was just like the stereotypical vicar on many a TV show.

'So, Claud,' he beamed, 'tell me how you've been.'

He was so warm and welcoming, it felt as though he and I had developed some kind of relationship, but my next admission was about to change everything.

'Well,' I breathed, 'I've actually got something I want to tell you.'

He just listened as I proceeded to tell him how I made my money; how I'd been making my money for a really long time. I remember the shock on his face; he literally didn't move, and stared at me for seconds that seemed to stretch to minutes.

'Well, Claud,' he eventually sighed, 'we're going to have to do something about that, aren't we?'

I nodded, unsure as to what he was going to say next.

'You're going to have to get a proper full-time, permanent job.'

I remember thinking as I left the pub that day: *This might actually be all right.* Though I was frightened of coming clean to the vicar, on reflection I think the buzz of knowing Jesus for the first time was blocking out everything else in my mind. I felt free of so much that had bound me, and confessing my deepest, darkest sins to a man I hardly knew and not being pushed away felt like a little taste of heaven. I didn't know it at the time, but in pursuing my thirst to know Jesus better, repentance was always going to be an inevitable outcome. Repentance – the activity of reviewing one's actions, feeling contrition or regret for past wrongs and turning away from such activities to become closer to God – is a hallmark of the Christian faith and evident throughout the pages of Scripture.

My journey to salvation hasn't been an easy one, but God is faithful and his word is true. There are those who celebrate my story as one of being protected by God in my darkest moments, quite literally keeping me out of prison, and transforming my path from one of abuse and destruction to freedom and hope. There are others who feel that I should be punished more severely for the crimes I have committed. All I know is that I relate wholeheartedly with Jesus when he says of the woman who anoints him in Luke 7.47 that 'her many sins have been forgiven – as her great love has shown. But whoever has been forgiven little loves little.' I have been forgiven much and I want to spend my life showing Christ's love to others the best way I can.

Bolstered by the vicar's gracious response and unconditional support, I clung to his very practical words: *You're going to have to get a proper full-time, permanent job.* My search for a legitimate job began immediately and I knew the only way to go about it was with God. I spent time reflecting on my life and prayed for change. I prayed for direction and wisdom, I prayed that I was making the right decision and that God would provide. After a lot of praying, I prayed some more. I was afraid of what leaving my old life behind would mean but was convinced Jesus had more for me; the desire inside of me to know him more was leading the way.

My entire life had involved crime in one way or another, so when I gave it up, I gave up life as I knew it. Whether it was visiting my brother in prison when I was just a small child or talking to my friends about crimes that I wanted to commit as a teenager, or *actually* committing crimes as an adult, one way or another my life had revolved around it. The hardest thing about giving up crime was actually starting again. I had to learn everything from scratch; how to live differently and do things legitimately. The good thing was, breaking ties with individuals I had previously associated with happened naturally. I removed myself as far from my old situation as I possibly could. One of the first things I did was change my phone number, and very few people knew where I lived, so it was highly unlikely that one of my associates was going to turn up at my house unexpectedly. To those who knew me on the streets I may have been nothing more than a criminal, but my choosing to change signified something else.

I looked at the small cheap mobile phone that I would receive all of my orders on; some people sell their trap lines and I've heard of such phones being sold for thousands and thousands of pounds. I imagine I could have got a lot of money for mine, but I knew that if I sold it I would be doing even more damage to society; I'd already poisoned enough people through my actions. No more. Similarly, I looked at the bag of cocaine I had lying around back home, and it was like I was seeing it with fresh eyes. Previously, picking up a bag of drugs would be like picking up your favourite jacket – you don't consciously see it as a jacket; it's just yours and it's always been there. Now it was as if I could see clearly for the first time. These were drugs and they were causing so much damage to myself and others. I was done with that old life. I had been filled with the inspiration to be something greater. I had fallen in love with something that I had always believed wasn't meant for me and made it my own. I knew my desire to pursue God had to be greater than my desire to sell drugs, so in times of loneliness or doubt I did two key things.

First, I would read my Bible and pray; I grew to trust God's direction for my life more than my own. I was moved to read of God's love for me and how he only ever wanted the best for me from the very start. Over time I began to learn what it really means to love; God's love has such great depth. It was through love that I found forgiveness; I believe the two are intertwined.

Second, I surrounded myself with people I knew would point me in the right direction. My vicar and his wife became my friends, then they became my family. We talked about everything. They treated me like an equal and I would go round to their house almost every day to hang out. Together we would discuss the Bible, and slowly their investment in me started to build my confidence in this new way of life. I also began making new friends through the church – people who seemed to have a genuine interest in who I was rather than what I could do for them. My life had already begun to change, and I could see it; I could see God providing for me every step of the way.

In Galatians 6.7–8 it says, 'Do not be deceived: God cannot be mocked. A man reaps what he sows. Whoever sows to please their flesh, from the flesh will reap destruction; whoever sows to please the Spirit, from the Spirit will reap eternal life.' *Finally* I felt I was sowing into my spiritual life; I knew I needed to take this approach to my work too. By the time the Alpha course had ended, I knew I didn't want to sell drugs any more, but it was more than that. I *couldn't*. The desire to do so had completely left me.

I started by asking where God wanted me to work. I also considered practical things such as working relatively local to where I lived at the time with my mother; I knew I would find such a gear-change hard and I didn't want to make life any harder for myself than it already was.

I soon found a part-time job as a barista, which I enjoyed. I worked the early shift, which meant that I had to be there for around 5 a.m., and without anywhere to park I had to walk there in the freezing cold. The contrast to my old life felt stark. I had gone from driving cars I could never legitimately afford to walking three miles to work every morning and three miles back in the afternoon. Still, I knew I was on the right track.

In order to supplement my income from the coffee shop, I eventually managed to secure a second job as a Christmas temp in one of the big supermarkets, where they eventually asked me to stay on as a permanent full-time employee. It was only through the grace of God that I managed to hold down this job for over three years, finally becoming an assistant manager there. I had never committed to anything for that long and for a while it felt like my story might end there. However, God was only just getting started.

With my role at the coffee shop meaning I had to work most Sunday mornings, I soon started attending the evening service at Holy Trinity Brompton, a church known by many as the place where the Alpha course was originally launched. Still filled with passion for my new-found faith, I volunteered at the church at any opportunity. As a result,

I got to know some of the ministry team really well and started to share some of my story with them. Eventually, it was mentioned to me that a job had become available at HTB's homeless shelter and I was encouraged to go for it. After praying about it, I decided to apply.

Though working at HTB Shelter wasn't without its struggles, it was undoubtedly one of the greatest experiences of my life in regard to how much I learnt about myself and about others. I confess, even with my own experience of poverty, I had somehow slipped into thinking that people who were homeless were somehow 'less than' me. It didn't take long at the shelter to realize I was wrong; we are all one step away from homelessness. I met one man who had once been the CEO of a large IT consultancy firm before he took his family on holiday and a terrible accident happened in which he was the only one to survive. Falling into depression, he lost his business, his income, his hope. He went from being a millionaire to homeless in a matter of months. And there are so many of these stories. I remember another chap who was really wealthy and bought a sports car to celebrate his success. One day when he was driving, he crashed the car and suffered some sort of brain damage that meant he couldn't continue with his career. He lost his job and his house, and ended up homeless. I soon learnt that it's not always the drug addicts and gamblers who end up on the streets; it's normal, everyday people who have often been living great lives before finding a few turns in the road cause them to end up completely homeless.

After working at the shelter for a period, I was offered a different role at HTB – this time as a church verger.

Through my time volunteering and then working at the church, I had started to sense a call to ministry, but I wasn't qualified to study, let alone consider becoming a vicar. The first person I discussed this stirring with was my mother, who was very supportive of my decision. I knew she didn't fully understand it, or even my decision to start going to Alpha, but she couldn't deny the drastic change she had seen in me. Her fierce loyalty towards me was once again a massive encouragement for me to move forward.

The second person I discussed a potential call to ministry with was my vicar, who helped me to discern it further. Deciding that I had indeed heard from God, the next step was to work out *how* I was going to study theology. The decision I had made to withdraw from academic studies so many years ago as a child had completely shaped my life as an adult, so it didn't seem likely that I'd secure a place on a course by any traditional means. Thankfully, the Peter Stream at St Mellitus College was just about to be launched.

Based on Acts 4.13, which says, 'When they saw the courage of Peter and John and realized that they were unschooled, ordinary men, they were astonished and they took note that these men had been with Jesus', the Peter Stream is described as a year-long course for those who 'have sensed a call to ordained church leadership, but have felt themselves, for whatever reason, excluded from the process of discernment, selection or training' (Diocese of London, 2020). When the opportunity arose for me to apply to the Stream with a view to becoming a curate in the Church of England, I jumped at the chance.

Working at a church and studying theology has been an adventure filled with both highs and lows. There's been many a time when I've felt very uncomfortable in my surroundings and questioned whether I'm really supposed to be here. Not so long ago, it seems, I was walking around Tooting with my mum, choosing my next toy to distract from the violence at home; then I was sitting in the halls in Kensington, being taught by some of the most renowned speakers in the country. *Am I really supposed to be here?* I have given the question great thought over the years and my answer is no, I'm not supposed to be here. By man's standards I wouldn't have even made it through the door, but by God's amazing grace I have a seat at the table. The Peter Stream has given me hope. It's provided me with the opportunity to take my understanding of my relationship with Jesus to a greater depth. At the same time, working out this theology in the midst of a dynamic church has proved another kind of education.

The people I have met through church have been more varied and diverse than I ever imagined possible when surrounded by lots of people in the world of drugs. Soon after I joined the church, I came across a man who was highly successful in his career and filthy rich. At the time I thought he was the man, proper 'big brother' material. Perhaps because of my background, I think he felt he could confide in me, so I soon found myself listening to him bragging about all the things he got up to behind his wife's back. Confused and conflicted about what this guy had told me, I went to one of the elders I trusted in the church. I had expected this of my old friends outside of church, but not in my new life.

'Claud,' the leader sighed, 'everybody you see in church – they are all here for a reason. We're all trying to figure it out. Everybody is flawed, everybody is carrying some kind of brokenness.'

Basically, if I was expecting perfection I should look somewhere else. This guy was broken. I am broken. Everybody is missing something. We've all got a spiritual hole that needs filling, and though I don't know what that looks like for everyone, I feel that everyone needs a piece of Jesus, and we'll be better people for it.

Though my calling to ministry came very early on, deciphering who I was going to minister to and where that would take place took a little longer to figure out. A large portion of my journey has consisted of me working with youth and young offenders. After working with the council mentoring young disengaged adults, I have since spent time visiting young offender institutions to speak to and come alongside the young men there. I also take part in a youth drop-in at the church where I am placed as part of my training; it's a small session that happens once a week after school and my focus is to use my time within the session to engage with the youth in a positive, non-judgemental way, which they'll hopefully find encouraging. In addition to this, part of my placement at the church consists of volunteering once a week with a charity that seeks to empower and assist disengaged young adults who are looking to enter into education or who are struggling to find work.

Regardless of the particular place or programme, nearly all of the young people I come into contact with remind me of myself in one way or another. I see the naivety in them, and it worries me; I want to show them that in this life we have choices and it's easy to make bad ones, but so much better to choose Jesus.

Like me, a lot of the young men I work with have severe underlying issues around confidence, identity and self-worth. I think one of the biggest problems that kids face nowadays is the constant pressure to be socially successful. From a very early age we're spoon-fed the lie that self-worth is derived from what we've got and not who we are. We're misled to believe that success is based on the balance of our bank account, that we have to achieve financial greatness or notoriety in order to be accepted. While I understand that security is important, it cannot be the anchor to our identity. When I see disengaged youth, I see a desperate need for change. We need to look for those on the fringes and walk alongside the less fortunate. Invest in others, find someone to mentor. Lead by example. Be community conscious. Love unexpectedly and remember our privilege is someone else's blessing.

Most of these young men have never had a positive role model in their lives; they have never had someone they can look to for good, trustworthy direction. I hope I can assist in equipping these young individuals with the tools that are required to thrive in this high-speed society and, in some cases, see them develop a long-lasting faith. In many ways, I feel I want to share with these young men the lessons I wish had got through to me when I was younger: that education is key; that they should study and equip themselves in a subject that they're passionate about, apply themselves, master a craft, develop their strengths, find a career. They need to choose their friends wisely, spend time with people who have qualities they admire, seek wisdom, get advice. I want them to know that they shouldn't be afraid to ask for help.

Ultimately, my prayer is that any contact I have with young individuals will ignite dialogue about Jesus and how he has changed my life for the better. I want to encourage people not just to hear about Jesus, but to get to know him. Actually get to know him, not just to know *of* him. Get to know Jesus in a way in which they've never known anyone before.

After some exciting but challenging years of study, I finally passed my BAP (the Bishops' Advisory Panel). I am now set to study for a further two years to become a priest in the Church of England. After this, I hope to plant a church in an area where myself and a team of others can make an impact. I believe Jesus can and will make a difference to a community. I hope to reach both disengaged youth and adults who are struggling to find a place within society, and be a helping hand in the decrease of knife crime and gang culture.

Regardless of where I am placed, however, with Jesus I am already far exceeding any expectation over my life and calling – both my own and that of others. At one point in time I thought I'd be a dealer until I got caught or killed. I never thought I'd make old bones, but here I am, approaching 40 and training to be a vicar. I never imagined any of this, but I guess Ephesians 3.20 is right. Jesus can 'do immeasurably more than all we ask or imagine, according to his power that is at work within us'.

THE HOLLOWNESS
THAT RESIDES DEEP
DOWN INSIDE CAN'T
BE BOUGHT, NOR
CAN IT BE FILLED BY
ACHIEVEMENT. I TRULY
BELIEVE IT CAN ONLY
BE FILLED BY JESUS.

CONCLUSION

From growing up in an abusive home to falling into crime and later finding Jesus, my journey has been a colourful one and I am so thankful to have had the opportunity to be able to share just some of my story with you. Of course there's a lot that's missing; there would be in any story of our lives. Some things we naturally forget, some things we choose not to remember. Something is always missing. But isn't that a true reflection of our lives?

Very few of us are brave enough to admit it, but deep down inside us all – at one point or another – there will have been that feeling that something's missing. We all have or have had a longing for fulfilment, and there isn't enough money or power or prestige in the world to fill that pit. The hollowness that resides deep down inside can't be bought, nor can it be filled by achievement. I truly believe it can only be filled by Jesus.

Jesus changed my life, but that doesn't mean I'm perfect or 'sorted' or always content. No, life for me has often felt like a struggle and I continue to learn many lessons the hard way. I still make plenty of mistakes and often get things wrong. My punctuality is terrible, my administration skills have plenty of room for improvement, and these are just the tip of the iceberg when it comes to my flaws. But by God's amazing grace, day by day I'm improving. Even being able to admit my flaws is progress – before giving my life to Jesus, my pride wouldn't allow me to do so. God saved me from myself and it's only through his salvation that I have been given the vision to see the error of my ways. I know that the Lord can use everything that has happened to me for his glory and that he has a plan and a purpose for my life and for yours.

It may be that you related to a lot of my story and that from a very young age your life has been filled with darkness and destruction. Perhaps you are walking down a road filled with emptiness. Maybe you are tired of your life. Maybe you desire change. I believe Jesus Christ is the door to life and I know that God is the God of new beginnings; his power is great enough to change anyone who is willing. We don't have control over a lot of what happens to us, but we do have control over how we react to it. Life is a journey and it goes by a lot quicker than we realize. We all have choices to make and I believe that for everyone there comes a point when we have the opportunity to make an absolutely life-changing decision.

So, do you want to change? God loves you and he wants to help you, so if the answer to my question is yes, then I encourage you to take the opportunity to invite Jesus into your life right now. All you've got to do is ask and God will change your life. Ask him right now to do for you what he has done for me and so many others. Ask him to change your life, to take away all that is rotten and make it worth living in Jesus' name.

BIBLIOGRAPHY

Diocese of London (2020) The Peter Stream (available online at: <https://london.anglican.org/support/ministry-and-vocations/christian-vocation/the-peter-stream>, accessed 3 January 2021).

Ditch the Label (2015) 'The annual bullying survey 2015: UK bullying statistics 2015' (available online at: <https://ditchthelabel.org/research-papers/the-annual-bullying-survey-2015>, accessed 4 January 2021).

Hudson, W. H. (1982) *Far Away and Long Ago: A childhood in Argentina* (London: Eland Publishing).

National Education Union (2019) 'The state of education: Child poverty' (available online at: <https://neu.org.uk/press-releases/state-education-child-poverty>, accessed 3 January 2021).

Office for National Statistics (2019) 'Domestic abuse in England and Wales overview' (available online at: <https://ons.gov.uk/peoplepopulationandcommunity/crimeandjustice/bulletins/domesticabuseinenglandandwalesoverview/november2019>, accessed 3 January 2021).

Runnymede Trust (2020) 'Race and racism in English secondary schools' (available online at: <https://runnymedetrust.org/projects-and-publications/education/racism-in-secondary-schools.html>, accessed 4 January 2021).

SafeLives (2020) website at: <https://safelives.org.uk>, accessed 3 January 2021).

THANK YOU

Sadly, my mother never lived to see this book come to fruition, but she was encouraging about my writing it and consented to me sharing our truth. She passed away in 2019, a week before my thirty-seventh birthday.

Living with the loss of my mother has been the hardest thing I've ever had to do. There's not a day goes by that I don't think of her. She was with me every step of the journey, so this isn't just my story; it's ours.

Thank you for always believing in me – for the unconditional love, the endless support and the relentless encouragement. I couldn't have asked for a better mother. I'll love you to my last breath, Mum. X

WE HAVE A VISION OF A WORLD IN WHICH EVERYONE IS TRANSFORMED BY CHRISTIAN KNOWLEDGE

As well as being an award-winning publisher, SPCK is the oldest Anglican mission agency in the world.

Our mission is to lead the way in creating books and resources that help everyone to make sense of faith.

Will you partner with us to put good books into the hands of prisoners, great assemblies in front of schoolchildren and reach out to people who have not yet been touched by the Christian faith?

To donate, please visit www.spckpublishing.co.uk/donate or call our friendly fundraising team on 020 7592 3900.